DODGEBALL
THEOLOGY

DODGEBALL
THEOLOGY

*a youth worker's guide to
exploring play and imagination*

BLAIR SPINDLE

Copyright 2012 by Barefoot Ministries®

ISBN 978-0-8341-5114-7

Editor: Audra C. Marvin
Cover Design: Arthur Cherry
Interior Design: Sharon Page

All Scripture quotations, unless indicated, are taken from The *Holy Bible: New International Version*® (NIV®). Copyright © 1973, 1978, 1984, 2010 by Biblica, Inc.™ Used by permission of Zondervan. All rights reserved worldwide. www.zondervan.com.

Library of Congress Cataloging-in-Publication Data: 2012908259

CONTENTS

Section One: Play and Imagination in Ministry — 7
    Chapter 1: The God Who Creates — 13
    Chapter 2: A Call to Imaginative Youth Ministry — 23
    Chapter 3: Christ Plays — 29
    Chapter 4: Wholeness in Life — 37
    Chapter 5: When Time Stood Still — 43
    Chapter 6: Peace in the Parentheses — 49
    Chapter 7: Finding a Place — 61
    Chapter 8: Alive with Joy — 67
    Chapter 9: The Dance — 79

Section Two: Practical Play in Youth Ministry — 85
    Chapter 10: The Perfect Player: Quest for Spiritual Maturity — 87
    Chapter 11: Hooked on Liturgy: Creative Worship — 91
    Chapter 12: Playful Devotion: A Table for Two — 101
    Chapter 13: Joyful Journeys: Trips as Play — 107

Choose Your Own Adventures — 113

Notes — 123

SECTION ONE
PLAY AND IMAGINATION IN MINISTRY

> It is not only possible to say a great deal in praise of play; it is really possible to say the highest things in praise of it. It might reasonably be maintained that the true object of all human life is play. Earth is a task garden; heaven is a playground.
> —G. K. Chesterton[1]

SECTION ONE

As the sun set over the lake on a summer Sunday evening, my two best friends in the world, Doug and Scott, waited with me for the rest of the youth group to leave the park. We had a master plan. We were curious. The lake where our youth group had been meeting occasionally that summer was a new, man-made lake on the outskirts of town. In the middle of the lake was an island, and in the middle of the island was a barn. We wondered what was in that old barn, but there was only one way to find out. There was no bridge or boat or motorcar to take us to the island. So we decided that night that we would wait until everyone was gone and then swim to the island.

Though the lake was man made, it was very large. But the old barn kept teasing us, daring us to dive in. We weren't on the swim team, but we all assumed we were in pretty good shape. We were involved in summer weight-lifting classes preparing for our winter sports. We were athletes and active, so we figured it wouldn't be any real problem to swim the distance. We found out soon enough that we figured wrong.

We laughed at each other as we stripped down to our boxer shorts. We all dove in together and were having a great time practicing our swim strokes, splashing each other, seeing who could outswim the others. It was a true moment of joy; a time of play in life that would certainly never be forgotten. This was the day we would finally find out what was in the barn. It was a great adventure. But then we began to get tired.

I distinctly remember the point in the middle of the lake where we stopped to tread water.

"Guys, I'm pretty winded," I said, knowing from their expressions that they felt the same way.

"No doubt," Scott said. "Maybe we should turn back?"

The way I remember it seems like slow motion. We all turned our heads together to look at the shoreline (cue the ominous, something-bad-is-about-to-happen music), and we realized we had made a terrible mistake. The shore was farther away than the island. We were stuck in the middle of this lake, treading water, doubting our endurance, and fearing we might sink into the abyss at any moment. Newspaper headlines of our demise flashed through my head: THREE CHURCH BOYS FOUND AT THE BOTTOM OF THE LAKE . . . IN THEIR UNDERWEAR!" Wouldn't my dad be so proud? We were in a real and serious situation. This adventure, which started out as a fun game, had turned into a life-or-death situation.

I don't recall exactly how the next part of the story happened. Over the years, the details have gotten fuzzy. But I do remember that one of us (we'll act like it was me and let Doug or Scott correct me if they ever read this book) made a remarkable discovery. For some unknown reason, I decided to test the depth of the water. I don't know why. Maybe knowing that you're going to drown in 10 feet of water rather than 15 would make a person feel better? As I held my breath and descended into the murky water, it hit me much quicker than I thought it would. Not the realization that we were doomed; the bottom of the lake. In fact, when I went under, my feet immediately touched down in the soupy muck of the lake bottom, and, well, I stood up. And I realized the lake was only 5 feet deep. I just stood up.

You can imagine the relief I felt, but it was news I wanted to hold onto for a little bit. The other guys still struggled to stay afloat. I stood with my feet on the bottom, paddling with my arms like I was still treading water and about to die. It didn't take long for the other guys to realize how shallow the water was. In a matter of moments, the fear gave way to a lake-muck war, and we walked the rest of the way to the island. When we got to the island, we had a decision to make.

SECTION ONE

> ## Choose Your Own Adventure
>
> ▶ A: If you want to open the barn door to see what's in it, go to page 114.
>
> ▶ B: If you want to leave the barn door closed and walk back to shore, go to page 115.

This has become one of those moments in life we all recall. We were really alive. Those moments are out there. We can choose to really live. Unfortunately, too many people are comfortable with the shore. They like being in the boat. They have no time for adventure. They have very little holy curiosity. They are armed with cute little quotes about what it did to the cat. Diving into a ministry or lifestyle of true celebration, laughter, and authentic play seems trivial, foolish, maybe even a bit dangerous.

A dodgeball theology remembers the words of Paul in 1 Corinthians when he calls Christians to be "fools for Christ." Kenda Dean mentions this and expands on it.

> Fun is good. Triviality is deadly. The word fun has its origins in the word "fool . . ." When fun leads to the foolishness of the cross, ecstasy flows from God's triumph over death and defeat. This is the tremendous mystery of faith that Christians celebrate: that joy springs from anguish, that love abounds in passion, that life comes from death, that hope hallows despair.[2]

I urge you to dive into the world of wonder. Refuse to put awe or passion or play on the bookshelf with the fat books of the smart people. Refuse to equate spirituality with somber seriousness and play with mindless triviality. We must remain committed to a robust theology of play—a dodgeball theology.

Dodgeball is a game that has been around for years. It is not difficult to understand, and anyone can play it, with any number of variations on the rules. Some people associate the game with pain, but it doesn't have to be that way. When we play dodgeball, it's a game in a designated space, with simple rules and a simple point. Two teams take colorful, gator-skin-covered foam balls and send them flying in all directions. The object is to hit and eliminate people on the other team while dodging or catching the balls that are being thrown your way. When all the players on one team are put out of the game, it ends.

Years ago, we experimented with our students, and for our game in the midweek youth program, we played fifty-two straight weeks of dodgeball and never played the same version twice. Maybe that's another book that needs to be written. For now, let's play dodgeball.

CHAPTER 1

THE GOD WHO CREATES

> It is possible that God says every morning, "Do it again" to the sun; and every evening, "Do it again" to the moon. It may not be automatic necessity that makes all daisies alike; it may be that God makes every daisy separately, but has never got tired of making them. It may be that he has the eternal appetite of infancy; for we have sinned and grown old, and our Father is younger than we.
> —G. K. Chesterton[3]

It was an old cassette with Scotch tape over the recording squares and a faded purple label peeling off that often stuck to the lid of the player when the red eject button was pushed with force. If you're over forty, you know what I'm talking about. The brown spooled tape was crinkled in several places and occasionally required the skilled precision of pinky fingers and pencil erasers to ease it back into place over the felt tip in the middle; which left the sound quality a bit warbled but didn't keep me from constantly playing it and sharing it with whomever could bear to listen.

CHAPTER ONE

The speaker on the cassette was some sociologist from back east somewhere named Tony Campolo who had this amazing way of making you feel really good and really bad in the same sentence. This particular message recorded has etched itself in so many ways into my memory, warbles and all. Campolo passionately spoke of a beautifully creative God who sadly goes unnoticed. He recalled a Buddhist monk who told him, "You teach your children to pray all wrong. You teach them to pray, 'If I should die before I wake.' It would be better if you taught them to pray, 'If I should wake before I die.'" According to this monk, no one seemed to be totally alive to life.[4]

These words began to shape me. The whole sermon still echoes in my soul. Really live. Relish moments. Become like children, who are spontaneous and joyful. Jesus knew that this was how the kingdom was to be lived. "We have a God who wants us not only to be freed from the burdens that keep us from enjoying life and living it intensely, he wants to fill us with an excitement, a childlike joy that enables us to live life with incredible enthusiasm, spontaneous joy."[5]

The most memorable part of the message was the end, when Tony talked about God's creative act. I loved to watch the faces of people hearing it for the first time. He said something like, "How did God create daisies? Like a child that is thrown up into the air and comes back down and says, 'Do it again!' That's how God created daisies. He created one and probably clapped his hands in excitement and said, 'Do it again!'"[6]

There is something compelling about a God like that. Robert Johnston, in his book *The Christian at Play,* says, "God need not have created a world that is beautiful as well as functional. But he did."[7] But we are so obsessed with functionality in the church that we often forfeit beauty. Our ministries, even our own spiritual lives, become experiments in pragmatism kept free from the wastefulness of childlike spontaneity and void of God's creative power. And our visions of the world and the kingdom of God become nothing more than nicely worded and well-maintained purpose statements with little attention given to the dynamic and living God who rides on the clouds, hovers over the waters, and creates something from nothing, order from chaos, and claps his hands in joy, saying, "Do it again!"

What our churches and ministries need more than flash or mobs or flash mobs is to dwell in the power of a God who creates. We the people don't have that power. We can play and imagine, but Christ's vision is authentically creative. John, the gospel writer, tells of Christ the creator with his well-loved opening:

In the beginning was the Word, and the Word was with God, and the Word was God. He was with God in the beginning. Through him all things were made; without him nothing was made that has been made. In him was life, and that life was the light of all mankind. The light shines in the darkness, and the darkness has not overcome it.[8]

Eugene Peterson calls John's gospel "a rewriting of Genesis 1-2. [It] is the creation story with Jesus Christ presented as simultaneously the revelation of Creator and creation . . . The Word spoke but continues to speak creation into being."[9] Imaginative youth ministry is a continual willingness to allow Christ to speak creation into being. This is always colorful, exciting, and vibrant with real life, like a game of dodgeball. It's not cutthroat competitive but rather pure recreation and, if done correctly, pure imagination. Dodgeball theology is a simple metaphor for the way we can experience God as the communion of youth and adults. It is water turned into wine and, indeed, more than can be consumed.

The problem with our modern, postmodern, and podern[10] ministries is that we often unwittingly allow the allure of consumerism

CHAPTER ONE

to entice us into functionality. We become products. We give way to institutions that, even with their good intentions, depersonalize us, reduce us to objects, role players. And slowly our souls, thirsty for living water turned to living wine, dry up along with the churches and ministries we lead.

Our churches and ministries need the mystical vibrancy coming from the creative Spirit of God. We need to submit ourselves to his creative work in us and in the world. We need to recognize and realize that the good news of Jesus is found in a touch of his hand: Behold, all things become new. We need to learn to play again; to engage in the adventure of life with Jesus Christ and to allow this to bring color, taste, and a newness of life into our own souls and into the souls of the people we minister to. We are created to be creative, and our ministries need to be infused with holy imagination and playful joy.

God used messengers like Campolo to form and call me. On a well-worn path to the altar I encountered the playful wonder of a God who spoke through a bush that burned without being consumed, calling even me to throw down the things that were mine and pick them up again after God transformed them. I felt my heart burning within me as Christ played with me on the road and opened my eyes when we dined together. I cried out, "Woe is me, for I am a man of unclean lips," and Christ himself touched me with cleansing. I clambered up the tree, and Christ sought me out and invited himself into my house. I opened the door, and we've been playing together ever since.

Answering the call of God on my life did not immediately compel me into vocational youth ministry. It did, however, continually ask me to say yes, regardless of the direction. Finding the will of God was important to me. I remember talking to my uncle about the will of God, and he told me to go in the direction I wanted to go until God closed the door. I wanted to be a history teacher, so that was the path

I took. What I realized is that God's creative touch is at work in our lives wherever we are, and it is much broader in scope than we can see at any given moment. God was preparing me.

The speaker at my college commencement ceremony was Tony Campolo. I was thrilled to be able to hear him in person. I sat listening to a masterfully crafted sermon challenging us to take our talents to the places that really needed them, refusing to settle for comfort, going where we could make a real contribution to the kingdom of God.

Sitting next to me was a beautiful young woman I fell in love with and eventually married. We whispered about Campolo and the ways he challenged each of us, and we agreed that we'd both be willing to go wherever God wanted us to go. Campolo ended his commencement speech with a story from his church back home. He loved to break into the rhythmic vocal patterns that are highly valued in the primarily black church he attended. He said, "One day, my friends . . . you're all gonna die."

Like I said, he could make you feel good and bad with one sentence.

He said, "One day you gonna die, and they going to throw you in a hole, kick dirt in yo' face, and go back to the church and eat potato salad."

I was really encouraged.

"On that day. Young people, as they gather 'round and tell your story. What will they say? What will they talk about? Your titles? Or your testimony?"

He continued for several minutes. By the end, tears ran down my face. Help me, God, to be true to the creative calling you have on my life. Help me to be an instrument of your imaginative, creative power in the world. Help me to have a testimony, not just some titles. That sermon, like the other, is imprinted even still in my mind.

CHAPTER ONE

I received two offers to teach history. One was in an upscale suburban school district with a great pay scale, upper-class students, and plenty of opportunities for titles. The other was in a run-down, century-old building in a small factory town comprised of predominantly working-class people. The salary was barely enough for one person to live on, much less two. But Campolo had stirred my imagination. God needed me to go. The door was open. I was going to be a history teacher. I was going to change the world.

It was May. We had been working hard in the garden where we were placed. Both my wife and I had agreed to lead the youth ministry at the local church we attended. We were scratching out an existence, investing in others, hoping to have that testimony we both dreamed about and birth testimonies into the lives of others. We planned a mission trip for the thirteen kids at the church. We were going to a small church to do some construction work and a kids' club. It was Tuesday, and we needed to reserve the vans, but I was stuck at school, so my wife and a friend made their way up the highway to pay the deposit.

Almost every seventh-grade student in my sixth-hour class was looking wistfully out the rain-streaked windows of our second-story classroom that day. I was a first-year teacher who insisted on weaving a philosophy of imagination and play into the normal curriculum. These kids knew the anticipated dodgeball game scheduled for that day would be canceled. They knew they would have to open their Social Studies books and get back to their chapter questions. They bemoaned the now soaked and slick playground as they trudged noisily back to their desks.

"We'll play tomorrow," I assured them all, which didn't make the chapter on the Intolerable Acts any more tolerable.

At the end of the day, as I waited for my wife to pick me up, on the chalkboard in my barely legible writing, I scratched these words: Never let weeds grow around your dreams. I thought about what I would tell the students tomorrow about living life without regret, about seeking testimonies rather than titles. As soon as I put the period on the sentence, I got a call from the office saying I had a phone call. On the other end of the phone, a friend from church told me about the accident.

Sadly, that dodgeball game would never happen for those kids. At the age of twenty-three, my first year of teaching was cut short when my wife of two years was tragically killed that afternoon. She was twenty-two years old. A drunk driver messed it all up. This was not the testimony I imagined we would have. This was not in the plan. Life, laughter, and play just kind of stopped for me. Everything seemed incomplete. And weeds crept into my dreams.

In those days following the accident, I began to contemplate what "wholeness in life" really meant. Perhaps, to fully appreciate joy, we must experience grief. Maybe something can never truly feel complete unless we experience some level of incompleteness. And what I realized in those wilderness days was that a life is made complete by pain and laughter alike.

My journey through grief led me to begin developing what I now call a dodgeball theology. This path led me to the open doors of vocational youth ministry in the local church. Down the lonely road of suffering I discovered new plateaus of joy. Like mountain trails leading to new vistas, the hike hurt, but the views at the top were worth it. Down that road I laughed harder than I thought I could and began to find that incomplete people and hurting teenagers needed the same experience of joy.[11]

CHAPTER ONE

Imagination and play were part of my curriculum in those early youth ministry days, but I had underdeveloped motives, and I lacked definition and articulation. Johnston says, "A theology of play… might be better understood as the Christian community's serious attempt to develop a fuller understanding of one of life's possibilities: the person at play."[12] There had been no serious attempt on my part to develop this fuller understanding. Perhaps that was why it was so easy to discard play, or at least apologize for it. Imagination and play in youth ministry are about wholeness in life. This means we embrace the things that are expected but not anticipated—things like tears and laughter, play and practices, joy and pain. N.T. Wright says:

> Comedy and tragedy both speak of things being out of order—in one case, simply by being incongruous and therefore funny; in the other case, by things not going the way they should, and people being crushed as a result. Laughter and tears are a good index of being human.[13]

Wright goes further to talk of Christ. He claims that, even though the early stories of Christ do not actually mention Christ laughing and only once mention him crying, they certainly hint at what was surely a reality for Christ, who was both fully human and fully divine. And Jesus was always going to parties. He ate well. He drank wine. He made up nicknames for his friends. He told strange stories. He did funny things. And he energized people.

> Wherever he went, people were excited because they believed that God was on the move, that a new rescue operation was in the air, that things were going to be put right. People in that mood are like old friends meeting up at the start of a holiday. They tend to laugh a lot. There is a good time coming. The celebration has begun.[14]

What kind of mood are we ministers in today? Do we live and do ministry as if Jesus is on the move and a good time is coming? Or do we acquiesce to the general sentiment of cynicism? What if we recaptured imagination and play in our youth ministries and churches? Chesterton's vision of God the Father as being younger than his children, his own creation, should be a challenge to us. Refuse to let the storms of life sour your disposition. Refuse to become cynical, cranky, and unaware of the creation that bursts forth all around us. Refuse to get so high and mighty holy that you prefer the one-time command, "Daisies, be!" over the excitement and joy of, "Do it again!" Let us all remember who we are and infuse our lives and ministries with play, joy, and imagination.

Steve Sjogren says it well. "My new motto is, Where the Spirit of the Lord is there is fun!"[15]

CHAPTER 2

A CALL TO IMAGINATIVE YOUTH MINISTRY

> It isn't so much that Jesus laughed at the world, or wept at the world. He was celebrating with the new world that was beginning to be born, the world in which all that was good and lovely would triumph over evil and misery.
> —N.T. Wright[16]

The search for a theology filled with imagination and play—a dodgeball theology—is one filled with questions.

- What does dwelling in the creative power of God look like in our ministries today?
- Why are we so quick to divorce practical spirituality from theology?
- What is authentic play and why is it so important?
- How can we sound the call to deep play and recreation for the church and for the world?[17]

CHAPTER TWO

We each see through our own lenses, and my eyes have been seeing things as a youth pastor in local churches for twenty years now. I type with my own fingers, so my prejudices are certain to seep through. But I imagine this quest is not solely for ministry to youth. Imaginative ministry is not age specific. We all were created, called to join with God in a mission of hope and restoration. Stamped on us from the beginning was the image or likeness of God.

Then God said, "Let us make mankind in our image, in our likeness, so that they may rule over the fish in the sea and the birds in the sky, over the livestock and all the wild animals, and over all the creatures that move along the ground." So God created mankind in his own image, in the image of God he created them; male and female he created them. God blessed them and said to them, "Be fruitful and increase in number; fill the earth and subdue it. Rule over the fish in the sea and the birds in the sky and over every living creature that moves on the ground."[18]

This concept of *imago Dei* (image of God) informs not only how we see and value creation, but it also informs us of our identity, which is a favorable gift from God. We the created ones are infused with godly imagination. We are formed to be part of the story we're telling. It's really a beautiful thing when you think about it. We aren't pulling random characters into our fiction but are living into the story of God, a story that climaxes with the God who steps through time and space into our own, nonfictional realities. In Christ we see wholeness again. The mystery of the Trinity reveals a God in relationship. We are again reminded of our origins. Though broken by sin, Christ can make us whole again while we work to restore others, all the while reminded on the journey that "God saw all that he had made, and it was very good."[19]

I know, I know. Things aren't all that good today. It may seem trivial to speak of imagination and play in our current condition. We see pain, poverty, and injustice all around us. As I write, there are multiple wars being waged in the world, and innocent people are suffering. As I write, devastation abounds. Natural disasters have wreaked havoc across the globe. As I write, brokenness rips at the seams of civilization. There are so many broken relationships, broken homes, and broken hearts. There is great cause for concern. There is little denying that things are not the way they were intended to be.

Scot McKnight writes in several books about what he calls "cracked eikons." Eikon is the Greek translation of the Hebrew word for image *(tselem)* and is McKnight's word of choice when it comes to describing the *imago Dei*. He explains:

> We are, the Bible tells us, eikons. Knowing we are eikons empowers us to love . . . We love, so the first three chapters of Genesis inform us, in four directions. We love God, we love ourselves, we love others, and we love the good world God has given to us. So, when Adam and Eve chose to go against God's good plan, they cracked that eikon. To be a cracked eikon means that our love is distorted in all four directions; we don't love God as we can, we don't love ourselves as we should, we don't love others as we ought, and we don't love the good world God gave us as we are designed.[20]

I stood with a group of youth pastor friends on a glass-bottom floor in the largest tower in the world, the CN Tower in Toronto. This floor, made completely of glass, allows for a person to stand and look straight down for 122 stories. It is breathtaking, beautiful, and terrifying at the same time. As I stood there looking down and pondering my own demise, one of the youth pastors from Alabama said loudly but to no one in particular, "You know, everything that's ever been made, broke!" We had a decision to make.

CHAPTER TWO

> ### Choose Your Own Adventure
>
> ▶ **A:** If you want to scurry off the glass floor and head down the elevator, go to page 116.
>
> ▶ **B:** If you want to talk all the youth pastors into jumping on the glass floor at the same time to see what happens, go to page 117.

I suppose there was great truth in those words. Even the good world that God made, his grand creation, broke. This is a deep theological issue that whole volumes have been written to discuss, describe, and define. For our purposes, it should suffice to say it this way: God created a good and just world, but sin entered the scene, and the world was no longer the way it was created to be. It was broken. And we the people—the ones created in his image to love God, others, the world, and ourselves—were indeed fractured, and the practice of our love has been rendered incomplete. The resulting chaos has brought us to where we are today.

Oh, but church: God is all good all the time and even still. We should clap our hands and giggle, *Do it again!* We should play in the midst of pain. There is hope in despair, light in darkness, peace in the storm, joy in persecution, restoration in brokenness and life, new life, the newness of life streaming into the world through the creative and re-creative power of Jesus Christ, and we ourselves are being restored to bring this creative touch to the world.

In our hearts, which spill over into our ministries, we should passionately long for things to be made right. As Christians, we believe this rightness and restoration are wrapped up in a theology of salvation through Jesus Christ, which is a robust, multi-faceted concept that doesn't fit squarely into one theory. We imagine this new life

God has for us. And so we should passionately seek and long to impart this hopeful, joyful, imaginative, and playful news to others, inviting them into the game.

CHAPTER 3

CHRIST PLAYS

> Play is an expression of God's presence in the world; one clear sign of God's absence in society is the absence of playfulness and laughter. Play is not an escape; it is the way to release the life-smothering grip of busyness, stress, and anxiety. (Playfulness is a modern expression of hope, a celebration of the flickering light of the gospel that plays with the dark by pouncing on the surrounding darkness like a cat toying with a mouse).
> —Mike Yaconelli[21]

> One of youth ministry's most important responsibilities is to sound the call to deep play and re-creation for the church and for the world.
> —Kenda Dean[22]

"You can't cancel the canoe trip." The leaders of the youth ministry were in agreement.

"I'm not canceling it; I'm tweaking it."

"What do you mean tweaking it? Is that the same thing as canceling it?"

CHAPTER THREE

There are always intangibles—things that are important to certain youth communities—and, for this group, the canoe trip was obviously one of those. The problem was that, to me, the trip just seemed lame and purposeless. They got in the van early in the morning, drove an hour to the river, floated for two to three hours, and then came home. I had bigger plans.

"This year the canoe trip is going to be called Thriver. We're going to go to a river that is four hours away, go forty miles in canoes, carry all our equipment with us, sleep on the open ground or whatever shelter we can find, eat whatever we can kill, and see who can do more than survive. Who will be the thriver? What do you think?"

Silence. Stares. Disbelief.

"Uh, did you say, no tents?"

Seventeen students decided they were up to the task. After much consideration we went ahead and threw some old tents in and carried them with us on the river. As soon as we started, the rain came. This was no drizzle. It was a downpour. The tents we brought were leaky. The kids slept with streams of water flowing over their bodies. (It just so happened that my tent was waterproof and comfy; go figure.) To this day they still report that night to be one of the most miserable yet memorable nights of their lives.

For eight years, this trip has continued, and the stories are numerous, whether good or bad. The reason we still do it? As Eugene Peterson might put it, to enlist the play of our students into the play of Christ. Theology is best learned on the river of life. Teaching is easiest when moments present themselves, rather than when we fabricate object lessons. It is the most meaningful when we are truly alive. Play can take us to those raw moments, and the astute teacher will never waste that kind of opportunity. Authentic play can teach us.

Youth workers were using moments of play to gather and teach adolescents before the term adolescence was even coined by G. Stanley Hall in 1904.[23] Even when youth ministry existed primarily to educate rural youth who had moved to the city to work, play was part of the curriculum. Youth camping experiences, fellowship gatherings, outreach events, and games (like dodgeball) are woven into the history of youth ministry. Play was and continues to be something teenagers desire.

Dodgeball is play, although for some, the game brings back welts of painful memories. Angst is a grown-up word that best describes my own childhood experiences with the game of dodgeball on the playground. I can still feel the sting on my face from the red rubber ball Corey Bradford sent blazing my way in third grade. So, as a metaphor, I'll be the first to admit that it is far from perfect.

But dodgeball has come a long way. The balls don't hurt anymore. It is still a game that requires movement and even agility, but it is one of the few games left that is still played for pure enjoyment. It is recreational. There are no organized high school teams requiring three hours of practice every day. There are no club leagues or traveling teams for adolescent dodgeball. (God help us all if there are!) There is no future to be had in professional dodgeball. You never hear about million-dollar signing bonuses, free-agent acquisitions, or salary caps for dodgeball players. There are no ESPN dodgeball highlights. Though some might disagree with this conclusion, I contend that dodgeball is still only a game.

A dodgeball theology is a colorful way of talking about a theology of play, which is an integral part of developing ministries that foster imagination and authentic play. It is important to who we are as spiritual people and as Christians. Too many pastors have equated spirituality with some kind of Puritan somberness or Protestant work code. The kerygma—the good news—is proclaimed like some kind of math problem that needs to be figured out. The concept of play is frowned upon. Just typing the word giggle makes me feel childish. What will the theologians think? We need to get serious. We need to be safe. We need a symposium to talk through these things. We need to be sure we follow the proper steps. What formula works best for you these days?

I'm not here with a formula. This ministry business is not so neatly bundled. It's a purposeful journey toward a certain destination, and the journey is sketchy at times. It is community, or even better, "a communion of saints"[24] who walk together, know one another, weep together, laugh together, and play together. Numerical growth is not a goal of communions but is often a result of them. This kind of growth is an obstacle that will have to be overcome. If a creative God is compelling, then a creative communion flowing with his power, grace, forgiveness, and intimacy will likewise be compelling. The family that plays together, stays together (and grows).

Eugene Peterson's book *Christ Plays in Ten Thousand Places* had me at hello. The title itself is compelling. Peterson believes the word play catches the exuberance and freedom that mark life when it is lived beyond necessity, beyond mere survival. Play also suggests words and sounds and actions that are intentional and meaningful renderings of beauty or truth or goodness.[25] He explains that his intent is:

> . . . to enlist your play (my friends and neighbors, my family and congregation, my readers and students) in the play of Christ. I don't have anything new to say: Christians already know the basics simply by being alive and baptized. We are already in on it, for Christ does, in fact, play in ten thousand places.[26]

Dodgeball theology is practical in nature, but it also affords opportunity for transcendence. Authentic play in ministry is important with many transcendent results. Johnston says,

> Though play is an end in itself, it can nevertheless have several consequences. Chief among these are the joy and release, the personal fulfillment, the remembering of our common humanity, and the presentiment of the sacred, which the player sometimes experiences in and through the activity.[27]

Resist the temptation to remove play from the curriculum. Imaginative youth ministry proudly sounds the call of deep play to the world and the church. Spirituality and play are not mutually exclusive. Depth and fun are not opposites. Often these elements are best when paired together. If we're not careful, we'll get cynical and serious. I like what Mike Yaconelli says in his book *Dangerous Wonder*: "Before you know it, you not only stop bouncing on your bed, you stop skipping, you stop playing hide-and-seek, you stop playing!"[28]

The stained-glass windows in our youth room that reached to the top of the cathedral told the story. Eyes were drawn automatically to multi-colored depictions of Christ as infant and shepherd, healer and teacher, servant and savior. It was a perfect and sacred environment and spoke the language of that mid-'90s postmodern generation. It wasn't a place for the trivial. Somehow basking in sun-drenched reflections of our sacred stories made games like Human Battleship or Poop Deck seem irreverent at best and certainly out of place in this kind of space.

So I drastically changed the midweek youth ministry program. In harmony with the room, we made all things deeply spiritual, which of course meant we put an end to play. No more fun and games. We instead inserted the creeds of the ancients and focused on upgrading our worship experience by using better visuals, turning down the lights, lighting candles, and developing outstanding, student-led worship bands. All these things seemed to fit the transitioning culture of high school students with their hunger for experience, image, and participation. Or so I thought.

As we progressed, the worship got better, the crowds got smaller, and something negatively affected the morale of our students. It was frustrating to feel like we were on the cutting edge of emerging trends, only to see that edge actually cutting away at our momentum. It left me constantly wondering what was wrong with these students.

Until Mat, a student who played power chords in a punk band, stopped me in the hall after church and said, "Hey, this sucks. It's no fun anymore. Why would I want anyone to come to this?"

My immediate cerebral response was to assess Mat's spiritual depth—or lack thereof—and perhaps his ignorance concerning the traditions of the church. Everything I was doing looked good in presentation and theory. It was done well. Maybe it would just take time to adjust to the change. But my gut feeling told me he could be right.

I went with my gut when Jimmy, one of our respected adult youth sponsors spoke up at a meeting and said virtually the same thing. "This approach we're taking is deep and spiritual and really enriching, but it's no fun at all. There is no joy. There's no laughter. Why does being spiritual mean we have to stop playing?"

This is a good question and important as we develop imaginative youth ministries. We desire for our students to be deep, grounded, and spiritual. We yearn for them to enlist their stories in the stories of Christ. We want them to be sanctified. We beckon them to delve into the deeper things of God. Authentic play and imagination are no hindrance to these desired outcomes. They are helps as we present a theology and example of faith that are full of color and life. We draw them toward the freedom that is in Christ.

I listened to Mat and Jimmy, and we started playing again. We continued with worship, creeds, and spiritual practices, but we never stopped playing. If those stained-glass windows could talk, they would tell of sermons and series, worship and passion, changed lives and renewed hearts. They might tell who stole the acoustic amplifier or who snuck into the catwalk during the Christmas musical. And they would certainly laugh as they tell of narrow misses from giant beach balls or packets of flying pudding. They would recall the real moments.

CHAPTER 4

WHOLENESS IN LIFE

> Life has been reduced to something less than itself. We as a church do not know how to play. In order to remove the blinders of our contemporary culture, we as Christians must listen afresh to the biblical witness. If we would only be attentive, we would hear Scripture proclaim that our play, like our work, is to be a God-given expression of our humanity.
> —Robert Johnston[29]

John records Jesus's first miracle in John 2:1-11, and in this story we begin to see the creative power of God through Jesus Christ. We begin to see a new vision of God, who calls us to use our imaginations, to live, to play, and to laugh. It shouldn't be surprising that Jesus's first miracle was at a wedding, nor should it surprise us that it was done at the request of his mother to save a friend (and herself) a lot of social embarrassment. After all, social disaster in a small town gets talked about forever.

CHAPTER FOUR

Weddings in Galilee lasted at least a week. Most of the people in that area lived on the edge of poverty. They ate two small meals a day. They had nothing. They had to ration. Life was strain and struggle. But when it came time for the wedding, oh boy, every family knew it was celebration time! They served three big meals for a week straight to all the guests and family who could make it. It was a time for them to forget temporarily about their poverty and just laugh and enjoy life.

Jesus had to know or sense, down deep in his soul, that a wedding was the best celebration of God's intended purpose for people in this world. It was a celebration of oneness. And isn't that, after all, the way we were designed from the beginning? Not only were we made and modeled after God himself, in his own image, we were also created, hardwired, designed to find purpose, meaning, and ultimate fulfillment outside of ourselves, in the eyes of something or someone else. That's why God made Adam and soon after Eve because God knew we needed community, companionship, and relationship. And since God is a relationship (Father, Son, Spirit) so should we be designed for relationship. This is life at its best.

We were created to be at one with God and at one with others. We were created to love God, love ourselves, love others, and love the world. This is one of the reasons people feel lonely. Maybe some of our students have a sinking feeling, a longing for something more out of life, a loneliness that is hard to explain but felt nonetheless. They were designed for real, non-coerced, unconditional relationships. They really need someone to invest and believe in them, to offer them a place where they can transcend their ordinary lives. They need a place where they can imagine a new world, a new life, something eternal, and so many of them just don't have it, which leaves them wanting and wondering if there's anything more to life. There's got to be something more.

So here we have a wedding ceremony that is now three days old, and the wine is almost gone. This is a major problem. It threatens to ruin the wedding. Having enough wine is a big deal, and it isn't about the alcohol, for drunkenness is rare. It is about hospitality. To run out of wine will make the wedding a social disaster, and since Mary seems to be in charge of the ceremonies, she can't bear for this to happen.

There always seems to be a problem. God created us, and we were perfectly at one with him and others, but then we chose—because we were free to choose—ourselves over God. With our sin we broke the oneness of our relationship and immediately began seeing each other as competition rather than companions, and we started dying, and soon we started killing to get our way. And it was, and in many ways still is, a big mess. Maybe that loneliness is really a feeling of separation or brokenness.

So Mary comes to Jesus, knowing he's pretty unique, knowing God has a call on his life, knowing he can fix things that are broken; and Jesus, in sympathy, at a small-town wedding, decides to act. Six stone jars, holding twenty to thirty gallons of water, used by the Jews to clean dust off the feet and hands for eating, are there at the feast. Jesus orders them filled to the brim, nothing but water, completely full; and immediately the problem is solved, water turned to wine, the wedding saved, and disaster averted.

What Mary knew, what John knew as he wrote this story, reflecting on it some seventy years after the crucifixion, is this: Jesus takes broken, messed-up things and fixes them. He takes lonely, unfulfilled, broken plans, wounded hearts, and interrupted lives and, in a touch, makes them right. In Jesus—his life, death, and resurrection—we are by his act and our choice brought back to God. We are at one with him and with others.

CHAPTER FOUR

Scot McKnight returns to his conversation about *eikons*. He writes,

> The gospel is designed to restore us in all four directions—in our love for God, for ourselves, for others, and for the world. This is why Jesus is the perfect Eikon: he loves God, loves himself, loves others, and lovingly observes and cares for God's world.[30]

An imaginative youth ministry with a dodgeball theology holds fast to this old and grand thought. Jesus can take your messed-up, lonely, separated life and change it in a touch to something amazing filled with color, flavor, and taste—oh, the taste, and not the cheap stuff; the good stuff, the best stuff; and not just a little, not a sip; 180 gallons worth, filled to the brim, sloshing back and forth, running over, more than could ever be consumed. We have so much to offer young people in the church.

If you're like me, your heart is heavy these days. How can we preach good news when the world is filled with death and tragedy? Many times in the past year I have wept for fathers who lost their daughters, mothers who lost their sons, children who lost their families, husbands who lost their wives. I have felt anger at corrupt, inadequate governments, lack of resources, lack of compassion from religious leaders, and a renewed feeling that our world is broken and that death is real and right around the corner. But I can love the God who has abundant resources. I can recognize that he created me and loves who I am. I can love others and help relieve a little pain in their lives. I can try to ease suffering the best I know how, and I can love the world by offering it the loving touch of a compassionate God. This is the essence of dodgeball theology integrated into an imaginative ministry.

Many of the students I work with need to hear a message of hope in the midst of their despair. So many of them are harassed by hurry, stress, pressure, worry, fear, and pain. The have lost confidence in the structures they once trusted. They need to be challenged by beauty and joy. They need to be surprised by the constancy of Christ. They need to be awakened to the realities of true fidelity, and they long for something real.

In a niche above the west wall of the Westminster Abbey in London stand ten recently carved statues of twentieth-century Christian martyrs. One of these is Dietrich Bonhoeffer, a well-known and beloved Lutheran theologian who was hanged by the Nazis in 1945 for participating in a resistance movement against Hitler's regime. Bonhoeffer is remembered for many things, but those who really knew him remember his affection for laughter, joy, and authentic play. These things were evident in his life and theology, both in the university and in his death-row prison.

In *The Christian at Play,* Johnston concludes with an inspection of Bonhoeffer and his tendency to embrace art, music, and play in his quest for wholeness and spirituality even while in prison. Johnston writes,

> Bonhoeffer's concern for wholeness in life—for faithfulness to Christ in both his work and his play—was evident even during his prison years. It was particularly apparent in the care he took to nurture his friendships.[31]

Johnston claims this as key to understanding the Christian at play, and I contend it is a goal in imaginative youth ministry. The goal is wholeness in life, which includes work and play, spirituality and laughter. Spirituality and play are not mutually exclusive. Not only can they occur together, they often do, resulting in rich and fulfilling benefits.

Perhaps there are pastors and youth ministry practitioners who, amidst the turbulence of a changing and often painful culture, are on a quest for authentic spirituality in the lives of their parishioners.

CHAPTER FOUR

However, in their desire to navigate these complexities of adolescence and cultural change, they have simply forgotten the importance of bouncing on the bed. There is no laughter ringing off the walls. There are no memories being made. Sacred space has become stale. Liturgy has become routine. Routine has become routine. We've neglected our responsibility to play. And by so doing, we have failed to form students into the Bonhoeffer-like whole Christians we desire.

Imaginative youth ministry has the opportunity, privilege, and responsibility to remind the church of the importance and spiritual benefits of Christian play. Youth ministry must struggle to delineate deep and relevant meanings for what it continues to do. Instead of discarding play and imagination from our curriculum, we must breathe life into them. We must know why we play, or we may never be able to really do it.

CHAPTER 5

• • • • • • • • • • • • • • • • •

WHEN TIME STOOD STILL

> The passion of play seizes us, therefore, not by force, but by ecstatically drawing us beyond our present reality into an alternative, non-anxious, delighted consciousness determined by God.
> —Kenda Dean[32]

Hiro Nakamura is a simple computer programmer for Yamagato Industries on the NBC TV series *Heroes*. One day while sitting in his cubicle, he blinks and stops time. He soon realizes he has the ability to bend time and space whenever he wants. All he has to do is squeeze his eyes shut and deal with the bloody noses. In a way, dodgeball theology offers us this kind of superpower. Imagination and play can bend time and space. Time can stand still.

The Greeks had different terms for time. *Chronos* is the ticking clock; time governed by orbits and spinning. Time that is seconds, minutes, hours, days, weeks, and years. *Kairos* is different. It is transcendent of *chronos*. *Kairos* represents God-ordained moments when heaven and earth intersect and time stands still. Authentic play brings *chronos* to a screeching halt, replacing it with *kairos*, if only for a short while.

These *kairos* moments can be some of the best windows to teach the deep truths of Christ, but the teacher has to be watching and ready. Our Thriver canoe trip became an annual event. We still take thirty to forty students every year on this outdoor adventure. It sounds trivial, but this book could not contain the spiritual lessons learned on this trip over the years.

On one particular trip, we were on a new river and failed to properly scout a good campground for the group of forty. In one day, our youth group paddled thirty-three miles, and by the time we finally did find a campground, we were exhausted. It just so happened that our campground was located in a swift stretch of water across from what looked like a giant cave. Some of us were, naturally, curious.

The first decision that had to be made was how we were going to get across the river. This was the swiftest part of the river, and the river was up. We stood on the shore contemplating the safest route across. We had a decision to make.

> ### Choose Your Own Adventure
>
> ▶ **A:** If you want to send one canoe filled with the strongest men with a rope to secure for the others to cross safely, go to page 118.
>
> ▶ **B:** If you want to head upstream a little and dive into the freezing-cold rapids and swim for it, go to page 119.

As we walked up to the mouth of the cave, we were amazed at how big it really was. A spring of freezing water ran through the cave, and it was big enough to fit our whole youth group. There were six of us who made the crossing, and we started working our way through. It was easy at first but soon presented us with challenges. The light from the opening disappeared, and we had to climb and crawl to continue our journey.

Thirty minutes in, we had not come to the end. It was getting more treacherous. Two of us had already slipped off some of the slick formations and would realize later we had some pretty severe scrapes and bruises. But we continued.

Forty-five minutes in, we finally reached the end, which opened up into a large room with a pool of ice-cold spring water. Weary from the trip, we all found a place to sit down. These are the kinds of teaching moments I'm looking for. I instructed everyone to turn their lights off and keep their eyes open. We had never experienced darkness like that. It was so real, so black, so consuming, and a bit terrifying. I encouraged everyone to pray. We took turns thanking God for this world and our friends and our lives and blessings and for him, who came and created and loved and provided. It was a precious and beautiful time. At the end of the prayer, I said simply, "Now, as we turn the light on, let it remind us that Christ is the light of the world, the light that shines in the darkness, and be glad!" The light came on, and we made our way out the same way we came in, but none of us were the same.

Our ministries and churches need to challenge students with authentic play. So many of our youth-serving institutions fail to provide the kind of recreation adolescents need. Chap Clark's assertions in Hurt: Inside the World of Today's Teenager are that these adult-driven institutions (families, schools, social organizations, and sports teams) charged with care for our children have forsaken their first assignment of caring for or nurturing the young. This is seen clearly in the arena of sports.

Sports and the lessons they teach have for years been important outlets for fun, play, and positive activities. But this has changed. Play

CHAPTER FIVE

is now considered work as student athletes realize that, to succeed, they have to commit to a year-round program and, to get a scholarship doing what they once loved, they have to do it so much that it just isn't fun anymore. So many students give sports up when they are allowed to choose for themselves. Clark says,

> It used to be fun to play sports . . . I cannot think of any other area of life in which we as a society have abandoned our young more thoroughly. From the time they hear "Play ball," they know that they had better come through and perform, even if they are only playing for fun.[33]

And slowly life leaks out of the teenage soul, leaving them abandoned and longing for more. "Sports . . . are no longer about fun, exercise, experience, and play. They are about competition, winning, and defeating an opponent. Sports are no longer child's play, they are a grown-up dog-eat-dog reality."[34] This is not the play we are calling for. We can't allow the result of play to compromise the goal.

A dodgeball theology claims that play in and of itself can draw players beyond the game, beyond themselves. Johan Huizinga, in his classic volume on play, identifies some of the main characteristics of play, the first being that play is not imposed as a task but entered into freely and offers freedom in return. Then Huizinga says,

> A second characteristic is closely connected with this, namely, that play is not ordinary or real life. It is rather a stepping out of real life into a temporary sphere of activity with a disposition all of its own.[35]

Peter Berger claims that play produces "signals of transcendence." The person playing goes by different time, and this different time is eternal; it transcends time, and this transcendence points us to the presence beyond time and space.[36] The presence is God who shows up in these moments of transcendence.

So in essence, authentic play can create alternative time. *Chronos* stands still, and an atmosphere of transcendence begins. For C. S. Lewis, play on several occasions pointed him beyond reality to a new reality of Christ. Perhaps this is best seen in his *Chronicles of Narnia* tales about children who, as they play, get lost in time and space. In Narnia, the kids are introduced to Aslan, the fierce lion who clearly represents Jesus.

I took my daughters to Hollywood's version of *The Voyage of the Dawn Treader* and was struck by the final scene when Aslan tells the children that the reason they have come to Narnia is to learn his name in their world and to know him better there. I began to imagine what imagination and play can do to the player.

This sounds a lot like Campolo's sermon. We only really live in the moments, the kairos moments designed by God. Everyone breathes, but not everyone lives. The result of the moments reminds us that there is much more to life than what we see. We are being beckoned. We are urged on to new realities. We are invited to join with Jesus in his kingdom work. So the moments on the river in the rain with a bunch of students can be so much more than fun or play or memories. They can be foundational in the formation of faith. And, as we recall the magic of these *kairos* moments, we can't help but whisper, *Do it again.*

CHAPTER 6
• • • • • • • • • • • • • • • • • • • •

PEACE IN THE PARENTHESES

> Are you tired? Worn out? Burned out on religion? Come to me. Get away with me and you'll recover your life. I'll show you how to take a real rest. Walk with me and work with me—watch how I do it. Learn the unforced rhythms of grace. I won't lay anything heavy or ill-fitting on you. Keep company with me and you'll learn to live freely and lightly.
> —Matthew 11:28-30 (MSG)

A little boy was out with his Dad on a Sunday afternoon, and they went by Chick-fil-A. "Daddy, let's go get some chicken nuggets!"

The dad responded, "Sorry, little man, we can't. They're closed."

The boy was disappointed. "Why are they closed?"

"Well, some Christian people feel that it's important to take one day off each week from selling stuff and making money."

The little boy paused then said, "Let's go to Taco Bell. They're not Christians!"

CHAPTER 6

Dodgeball theology is committed to a robust Christian practice of Sabbath keeping in new and life-giving ways. Sabbath, like a parenthesis in a sentence, interrupts the regular order of things. Youth ministries governed by God's holy imagination for his people are comfortable with interruptions. We need a regular pattern of pauses in our lives and our ministries, but the art of Sabbath is lost on our generation. Recapturing the poetry and practice of Sabbath is like the little boy who put his finger in the leaking dam. As life slowly seeps away from us in our busy, demanding world, we need a holy presence to plug the holes in our souls, allowing for a continual refilling without fear of the dam breaking.

For twenty years I have been spending much of my time with teenagers—in churches, vans, schools, parks, missions, rivers, and mountains. I've learned to start asking different questions than "How are you doing?" because I always get the same answer.

"I'm really tired."

Or, "I'm really busy."

Gone are the carefree days of youth. Sadly, our kids are hurried along to adulthood. David Elkind bemoans the loss of childhood.

> The concept of childhood, so vital to the traditional American way of life, is threatened with extinction in the society we have created. Today's child has become the unwilling, unintended victim of overwhelming stress—the stress borne of rapid, bewildering social change and constantly rising expectations . . . We do our children harm when we hurry them through childhood.[37]

This does not slow down when they reach adolescence. Our kids are targeted as consumers. They are used like products. They are sexualized by society. They are in high demand. They are stressed. Their schedules are packed. This is one reason that event-driven youth ministry is becoming obsolete. Trying to plan some kind of new event in youth ministry by working around the schedules of adolescents is like trying to eat pudding with pantyhose on your head, almost impossible and really messy (spoken from experience). Anything we try to add, regardless of how noble our motives, can become anti-productive in the forming of holistic Christians. It will just add to the noise in their lives.

We are all so busy accumulating things. We own things, have things, like things, and want things. Our students develop the patterns early. They have or want things like designer clothes and purses, shoes, cell phones, iPads, iPods, iTouches, computers, cars, good grades, exemptions, scholarships, savings accounts, credit cards. Why are all these things important? The free-enterprise machine has convinced us that we can't be productive without them. And in more ways than one, if we're honest, we show by our frenetic actions that we just don't trust in the wealth of God. We live in what Walter Brueggemann calls "the bad dreams of scarcity."[38] We worry that we won't have enough.

In *Mandate to Difference*, Brueggemann has written several articles that expound the ongoing need for Sabbath. His expositions have profoundly influenced me, and I only offer summaries. Pastors and youth pastors alike could benefit from reading his essays in their entirety. Brueggemann claims the reason we violate Sabbath (and I'm not talking about breaking the rules here) is that we "don't believe in, trust in, or count on God's abundance."[39] Our people are worried. Teenagers are afraid for their future. They don't act like they're aware, but if you really get beneath the surface, you will begin to understand that their conception of the future is not always bright. Trust is difficult for many of the young adults and teenagers I work with. They don't trust their own parents, much less the provisions of an unseen God. To believe that God will provide is a large step. However, failure

CHAPTER 6

to take that step only increases their anxiety. We need Sabbath. We need Christ. We need a cure for the escalating worry that abounds.

The word Sabbath comes from the original Hebrew word Shabbot, meaning "to cease." It means we pause or break from our normal habits. So a Sabbath is a ceasing from work, from commerce, from any habit that affects the natural world, from the normal comings and goings of life. And in the parentheses, there is peace.

We find the first account of Sabbath keeping in a peculiar story in the sixteenth chapter of Exodus. The story finds the Israelites in the desert feeling desolate. And they begin to grumble. This particular story takes place before the trip to Sinai, where God will speak to Moses with the law. It is the story of the people of Israel, who have quickly forgotten the agony of the slavery they used to live in. Moses and Aaron, with God's help, have freed the people from this bondage in Egypt. It was in Egypt where they were forced by Pharaoh to work all day, every day, gathering straw, making bricks, meeting quotas, and bowing to the imperial rule. It was a miserable existence ruled by hard men who demanded hard work and offered no reprise.

They are now free and have witnessed amazing things in the process. But now they are in the wilderness, a barren land with no institutionalized meals or imperial order. There are no fierce whip tips slicing their backs, but there are also no guarantees of safety or nourishment. They are afraid there won't be enough for them to survive. They are convinced there will be a shortage. They quickly forget about the torment in Egypt, only remembering the good things. Grumbling they exclaim, "If only we could go back to Egypt," and, "Moses, you brought us to the wilderness to die of hunger."

Here's the good news. God meets all of their complaints with all of his abundance. Brueggemann says, "God's abundance always outruns our expectations and our categories of explanation."[40] Bread is given. Not just boring white loaves from the oven. A creative God imagines and plays. This is crazy-fun magic bread that falls from the sky, and lots of it. Isn't that odd? Isn't it great? God will always answer the bad news of not having enough with the good news of having more than enough. Of course, God's more than enough comes on his terms and not ours. The creative power of God offers all that the creation needs but offers it with stipulations. There's always one tree we just can't eat from.

God says (my paraphrase), "Gather as much as you all need. Distribute it. Make sure you have enough. But don't try to save it, and don't you dare acquire a big surplus. Just take what you need and use it." But the people don't believe in, trust in, or count on God's abundance, so they hoard it, and it is rotten with maggots in the morning.

Brueggemann explains, "A surplus of anything gathered in anxiety will contradict God's abundance."[41]

Here's what happens next. God commands them to gather and store enough for two days so that on a Sabbath the people can rest in the abundance of God. Manna is very truly daily bread; it doesn't keep for two days. So the people are probably concerned at the nature of this imperative, knowing that a two-day supply of bread will be rotten. They have to take God at his word, and when they gather enough for the Sabbath day, the bread doesn't rot!

So it comes to pass that gathering is completely unnecessary on the Sabbath. It is the day that is simply a gift of more than enough, and it requires no energy from the people. The pattern still holds today. Sabbath requires a complete confidence in God's provision. God wants us to have confidence in him, and practicing Sabbath reminds us that God will add all these things to us as well.

Jesus understands the reasons for Sabbath. He modeled for us a life of total dependence on God and complete trust in his abundance.

CHAPTER 6

We need to model this for our churches and students. Pastors, someone needs to imagine something different from the current realities of culture. Will you offer a parenthesis to your people? Do you practice it yourself? We all need to learn to trust in the resources of Christ, realizing that we have all we need. A dodgeball theology boldly offers rest from the regular routines and peace in the parentheses.

A second and more official call to Sabbath comes in Exodus 20:1-17, which is the familiar account of the law given to Moses. We all know exactly who this God of Israel is and what his intentions are, but what about the people in the story? How do they know who this God is? They have no real access to the scrolls. Most of their knowledge of Yahweh has been handed down through oral stories. They trust in the stories of their ancestors, so to complain about the lack of food is perhaps a bit more understandable. And we know that God has met their complaint with his abundance by sending magic bread from the sky and chirping quail. And we know now that this is the kind of God he is. But the Israelites aren't too sure.

Out in the wilderness, the people approach Mt. Sinai and notice it is alive with God's presence. I'm always kind of seeking God's presence. As a pastor, I want my people to experience God's presence like it's something warm and fuzzy. It rarely occurs to me that I'm asking people to do something dangerous. God is not warm and fuzzy, and in this story, his presence is downright scary. It isn't user friendly or seeker sensitive. The people at the foot of this mountain won't be cheerfully singing, "I have a friend in God; I call him friend." What kind of friend will this God be? Why is Moses even messing with this God? Surely this isn't the same God who parted the sea and provided bread.

Then this strange, terrifying God speaks, in Exodus 20:2: "I am YHWH—the Lord Your God" (a strange name with no vowels that Jews won't even speak aloud to this day), and then he lets them in on the secret, "who brought you out of Egypt, out of the land of slavery." This is the same God who did incredible things on their behalf! Is he a God to be trusted?

Most of us know what happens next. The same God who freed the slaves gives ten laws—ten commands—to the people. Brueggemann's exposition of this text is intriguing, and I offer a quick summary. Three times God speaks about the love of God, and six times he speaks about the love of neighbor, which is why, later, Jesus is able to summarize the great commandments the way he does. Love in this setting is a word that basically means "binding agreement" or simply "honoring commitments." Three commands to love God: No other Gods, no images or idols, and no words that degrade or reduce God in any way. Six commands to love neighbor: Parents, killing, committing adultery, bearing false witness, and coveting. These are summed up in the two greatest commands, according to Jesus (love God, love neighbor). But notice this. Right in the middle of them, BAM! (I had a doctorate professor who said that all the time). BAM! The longest commandment; the one that looks back on the love of God, who rests, and at the same time looks forward to the neighbor who needs to rest.[42]

The Sabbath imperative is unique. It is to be different from other days. Other days are workdays, and in many ways they, are devoted to our own well-being. But this day is devoted wholly to God. Holiness is always about setting things apart, and in this instance, it is a day—a moment—when *chronos* becomes *kairos*. It's a day for stopping work, pausing, ceasing. It's not really connected to going to church or corporate worship. God is acknowledged when we stop being so productive. It's a call for everyone to stop. It's a call that was modeled by God himself. God wasn't just constantly creating things. He took a break. Likewise, we are designed to be productive and constructive, but we must also learn to be recreated, to rest, and to find peace in the parentheses if we want to truly be what we were intended to be.

So we learn a little more about this God. He spent six days creating (working), and then he rested. Sometimes our students need to know that our God is a God who neither slumbers nor sleeps. But other times they need to know that he is a God who rests. These apparent contradictions have a message of hope for this generation. Producing things is costly; creativity wears on you; giving yourselves to others is a tiresome task. Our students are constantly being called to produce. They are pressured to succeed on standardized tests, to exceed the once treasured 4.0, to prepare all summer for the season, to get stronger, faster, better at everything. And, impressively enough, they rise to the challenge. Teenagers today are truly amazing creatures. But they need to rest and be replenished.

In Exodus 31:17, God says to Moses, "It is a sign forever between me and the people of Israel that in six days the Lord made heaven and earth, and on the seventh day he rested." And then this conclusion: ". . . and he was refreshed."

This is an amazing statement, really. God was refreshed. Again, Brueggemann's exegetical work is my source. He identifies the Hebrew word translated as refreshed as both a noun and a verb. It is the word *nepheshed,* and it can mean both the soul or self, and refreshed or replenished. It's a natural cycle. "Our souls/selves (*nephesh*) are drained and need to be "re-nepheshed" or replenished."[43] And you guessed it; Sabbath is a time for being re-nepheshed, which allows for a recovery of your full self and stops the life-leaking patterns we so easily fall prey to, even in the church. We are replenished by withdrawing from the things that drain and exhaust and deplete—even if they're good things!

Dodgeball theology calls us to replenishment. Sabbath reminds us all that we have limits. Like a battery that runs out, your true self, your soul, your nephesh has limited energy. We have already established the *imago Dei*. We are created in the likeness of God and wired in certain, unique ways. We are often depleted, so we must pause, go to a safe and ordered place, our own tabernacles, and allow the Spirit of God to touch down in our lives. In Sabbath we render ourselves available for the refreshing that comes from a holy God. It is holy time and space. Brueggemann says it well: "It is the truth of our life that we are meant for restful restoration."[44]

So how does a ministry practically call people to Sabbath? Theology is fine but is rendered impotent if not applied to daily life. The first thing we all need to do is simple: Don't stress about Sabbath! That just wouldn't make sense. We don't view this as a legalistic command but rather a gift to be lived into.

We all, teenagers and adults alike, are overly busy and stressed. Juliet Schor's classic book of the '90s, *The Overworked American*, reported increased work hours, decreased sleep, and decreased play and authentic recreation. We know this to be true by experience. Second, authentic rest is found in Jesus Christ and in the gift of Sabbath not because we have to take some certain twenty-four hours off but because we can set aside time for Christ, and Christ calls us to rest.

When you read Peterson's paraphrase of Jesus's words from Matthew at the beginning of this chapter, how you feel? That passage beckons me to take time off and rest in him. It urges me to create arenas where students can experience rest in my ministry. Have you added this to your curriculum? Play offers us a chance to invite students into the parentheses of life. It can be that moment. It can allow us to teach timeless truths. I'm convinced that Sabbath is a gift waiting to be unwrapped in our ministries.

CHAPTER 6

Dos and *Don'ts* are always dangerous. But for the sake of practical theology, I offer some ideas about what Sabbath looks like, what we can do to honor it in our day and age, and what we still *shouldn't* do.

DO:	DON'T:
Be with the community. Solitude is a valuable practice, but the community ushers Sabbath in. How can our worship services be faithful to the practice of Sabbath?	**Go through the motions.** Godly rest cannot be coerced. Obligatory religious ritual will quickly and surely drain your soul of life.
Sleep. Don't be so over scheduled that you can't just sleep a little. Replenishment requires authentic rest. Discipline your time to allow for sleep.	**Sleep all week.** Sabbath rest is predicated by a week of work and productivity. Sleep—and lots of it—should be encouraged on Sabbath, just as work is encouraged throughout the week.
Worship and sing. This has been part of Sabbath keeping throughout the centuries. Gathered or scattered, we lift our heart songs to God. We engage in a two-way conversation with Christ.	**Perform or entertain.** This is one of my main contentions with worship at many of our churches in America today. We sit back and allow people to perform for us, or we perform for others.
Participate in communion. The Eucharist is a beautiful way to practice Sabbath. The act of remembering Christ at the table and his holy presence in our lives can replenish us.	**Participate in cynicism.** While there is so much about life, the world, and the church to be disparate about, refuse to do it at least for these few moments in the week. It might spill over into the rest of life.
Pray and read Scripture. Any of our typical Christian practices should be accentuated during Sabbath since communion with God is the ultimate goal. After all, it is God who replenishes us, not the moment.	**Compartmentalize your life.** Don't reserve Christian practices for one segment of your life. Increased focus on these things for Sabbath does not mean they are absent on other days.
Hike, bike, walk, and enjoy art or nature in leisurely ways. Take time to live deliberately. Stop and enjoy the natural world. Breathe deeply. Appreciate the fine things in life.	**Be productive.** Take moments each week to stop being so productive. Don't work. Don't alter the material world if at all possible. Just take time to be.

DO:	DON'T:
Kiss your loved ones. This has always been part of the equation of Sabbath. The Hebrews encouraged married couples to be intimate on the Sabbath. Maybe not such a good recommendation for teenagers, though.	**Use other people like commodities.** Don't unwittingly engage in consumerism when it comes to other people. In small ways, we exploit people when our engagement with them is for our own good.
Visit the homebound. Spending time with people in their own homes can reenergize our lives and the lives of people who are less fortunate.	**Spend money.** What if, each week, we decided we would take some moments to refuse to be part of the system? Abstaining from the consumption process might offer peace.
Invite others to your table. Enjoy good company, good food, and good drink. Recline at the table. Don't be in a hurry. Look deeply into the lives of others and let them get a glimpse into yours.	**Stay head down in technology.** Take a break for God's sake. Intentionally turn the gadgets off and focus on who you really are in the light of Christ's revelation in your life. You might be surprised.
Get quiet, meditate, read, and pass the peace of Christ. Practice these internal acts of spiritual formation. Allow the good news to go deep into your soul. And be willing to say to others, "The peace of Christ be with you."	**Be consumed with worry.** We all need to take time out of our lives to really let the fears and concerns of the world fall away from us, if only for a little while.
Play and laugh. Play a game. Tell a joke. Laugh from your belly. Take a break from all things overly serious. Be willing to be silly. Have some fun and let God seep into your soul.	**Be stuffy and serious.** You may need to just force yourself to smile every once in a while. You may need to get the courage to start bouncing on the bed again. We need times in life to unwind.

Dodgeball theology urges individuals as well as whole ministries to take seriously the need for renewal and replenishment. Sabbath is a biblical model that best supports this. It calls for ministries to seriously reconsider the programs we offer and the reasons for them. It is not a trivial endeavor.

Dean and Foster have much to say about time and space in youth ministry. In *The Godbearing Life,* the authors call for youth pastors in Godbearing ministries to take seriously the biblical call for Sabbath. "The question for Godbearers is not should we but how shall we reclaim Sabbath keeping in ways appropriate to our time and context?"[45] Dodgeball theology asks these questions, and our prayer is that we find ways to reinstate the practice of ceasing called Sabbath.

CHAPTER 7

FINDING A PLACE

> Sacred space provides room in our lives and in the lives of our youth for godly play, an intentional contrast to the work of our jobs, our schools, or our household chores.
> —Ron Foster and Kenda Dean[46]

One thing that is often overlooked in ministries today is the power of space and environments. Sacred space has been important throughout the history of God's people. The Genesis account speaks of space. The garden itself becomes symbolic of that place where creation is as it should be. There is a place where we are at our best. There is a place where God will meet us. There is a place where Christ plays and we learn to love in all directions. Dodgeball theology is concerned about the power of place, sacred space, and holy ground.

One of my favorite scenes in the Disney classic *Remember the Titans* is before the first big football game. Coach Boone (played by Denzel Washington) meets his friend from the school administration at night at the football stadium. The coach has been hired to coach one of the first racially integrated high school football teams in the south. He has done all he can do to bring the white players and black players to a place of trust and equality. They have trained and prepared and are ready for the first game.

As the coach strolls onto the deserted field with lights shining down on the chalked-up turf, he just stops and breathes in the moment. Silence. Then he says simply, "Yeah, this is my sanctuary right here."

He crowns this place as sacred. For him, it is something set apart. "All this hatred and turmoil swirling all around us, but this—this is always right. Struggle. Survival. Sometimes victory. Sometimes defeat. It's just a game, Doc. But I love it."[47]

Sadly, the football coach in this movie has a better concept of sanctuary than many pastors and parishioners in the Christian church today. A sanctuary is a place set apart. It is an environment people can enter as they are and transcend the normalcy of life, if only for a short while. There is nothing magical about the space itself except that it is a designated place for the intersection of heaven and earth. It is holy ground because God is present. It is a burning bush, a tent of meeting, a holy of holies, an ark of the covenant, a temple, a river of baptism, a mountain of transfiguration, a cross, a tomb, an upper room.

Our church sanctuaries can be sacred space if we humble ourselves enough to make room for the presence of God. Our youth ministries can be environments that summon teenagers to new realities with Christ. Our own homes, our offices, our kitchen tables, our backyard nooks can become places that are consecrated to and for all things spiritual. Our own hearts and lives can be consecrated in much the same way.

There is value in considering the environment of our ministries. This consideration includes holistic assessment of the physiology that makes us what we are. What is the climate of our ministries? What do the physical, social, emotional, and spiritual elements of our ministries say to people when they enter our ministries? Youth ministries should strive to find new ways to create climates that are conducive for spiritual growth, acceptance, and multi-directional love. Pastors should be concerned with the current morale of their churches, small groups, and programs.

I tend to agree with Foster and Dean when they assert that space is more likely to become sacred when it is consecrated for joy and even purposes of godly play. We're not talking about silly games. Make no mistake; imaginative youth ministry is more than brainless games and fun. But even in worship, we see Christ at play. Worship is more of a dance than an equation. Sacred space means our ministries are designed in such a way that, even as people enter the doors, they realize they have stepped into a place where people truly love a Creator, love themselves, love each other, and love the world in which they live. And fun and games are not unimportant. Too many people divorce joy from holiness and are left with a passionless, bland, and colorless religion.

One important characteristic of play is that the player tends to get lost in playing and, by doing so, has broken through the prejudices, anxiety, and angst that come naturally to our people in this production-oriented society. We need sacred space to provide those *kairos* moments that point us to the God who is beyond our senses.

One of my explicit goals in youth ministry has been to create a loving, emotionally safe, playful, and accepting environment. This has not always been easy. Students are so diverse, and the nature of adolescence is to develop values based on perceptions of key influencers. This game of looking to other people for worth often leads to exclusionary actions by groups who have determined that, for whatever reason, they are not on the same social levels as their peers. Creating the kind of environment desired means finding ways to level the playing field, and one great way to do this is through authentic play.

This environmental approach to youth ministry was modeled to me first by a volunteer youth worker named Brenda. The first time I entered that church, I was drawn in by laughter, love, and acceptance. There was nothing overtly seeker sensitive in the setting. The congregants were unapologetic about their belief in Christ and what that entailed. But I was not drawn to their call to believe as much as I was to their invitation to belong. Their approach to faith and to life was contagious. It was fun. Their church and homes were open. You could never predict what might happen next. They weren't interested in theological treatises, but they were intent on family cohesion. This was a sacred place for me. A family I wanted to be part of. It was a place I kept going back to and, over the years, a place I've tried to model my subsequent ministries after.

The messy part about ministry with people is that it is ministry with people. People are not so neatly packaged as to fit into our programs. There is no single, perfect ministry model out there that will work without fail in your setting. What will work in all of our settings is creating an environment where people genuinely feel loved, validated, accepted, and treated as equals. When these things are in place, we will start seeing people submit their stories to the story of God and enlist their play as the play of Christ.

Jerome Berryman, a religious educator and child development consultant, published a study in Christian education in the early 1990s entitled "Godly Play." He talks about the importance of place and environment:

> When we walk into a room, the colors, the arrangement of the furniture, the odors, the noise, the taste on the tip of the tongue,

the shape of the room, and other perceptions combine to "speak" to us . . . This is why the church has always been careful about the arrangement of space within the worship area . . . The environment is at work communicating even when we are not attending to communication.[48]

Berryman's religious education experiment included creating a place—an actual room—where Christian education for children could be experienced in tangible yet imaginative and creative ways. His space included symbols, art stations, altars, images, candles, and carefully arranged shelves and lights, all intended to teach specifics and create an educational and specifically Christian climate. He wanted the environment to communicate the desired message and foster creativity in the minds of students. He believes much of what we teach is modeled by the environment and not necessarily contained in discourse.

He says, "When we ask children to get dressed up and come to a special place on a special day, we must be careful, for we are teaching something. The question always is, What is the hidden curriculum? Does it match what we intend to teach? Do the spoken and the unspoken lesson teach the same values?"[49]

As I type this I'm thinking about the pencils stuck in the ceiling of the youth room. Our video game units are in disarray, there are Coke stains on the carpet, the sound booth is a disaster, and you don't even want to see the storage closet. So I'm feeling a bit convicted. While I believe we have created a positively Christian environment and accepting climate in our ministry, I need to re-imagine what message we are sending even with something as simple as the physical environment.

I do not necessarily advocate a seeker-sensitive approach to environment. People come to church expecting something spiritual to

CHAPTER 7

happen. But we could learn some lessons from the seeker-sensitive movement. We need to think about what our space teaches. We need to think about how our people perceive it. We need to realize that everything we do teaches what we believe. We need to create environments for spiritual growth in our ministries.

CHAPTER 8

ALIVE WITH JOY

> Laughter is the hand of God
> on the shoulders of a weary world.
> – Author Unknown

Warning. Live animals were injured and/or killed in the following story.

High school guys have a tendency to be, well, gross and cruel; even the good, Christian ones. At the church I grew up in, the legendary story is told about a pool party at the house of a guy who lived on some land outside of town. The youth pastor planned to have the whole group out to this house for pizza and swimming, just a typical youth group get-together. The guys in the group decided they would come out early to help set up and see what kind of trouble they could get into, and, most importantly, they really wanted to gross out the girls when they came later that evening. (It's no wonder they had trouble finding dates.)

CHAPTER 8

As they begin exploring, the news spread that there was a dead animal in the trashcan. Upon investigation, they realized it was a small possum, and they hatched a perfect plan. They would make this dead possum look as gross as possible and do something with it to really freak the girls out. Road kill has to be high on the gross-out scale.

So they retrieved the possum and decided it would be much more effective if they burned it to a crisp. They carried it out in a field. They placed it on the ground. They said some ceremonial words over it. And then they doused it with lighter fluid and set it on fire.

At this point they learned a lesson they will never forget. A possum, when threatened, will play dead, thus the phrase "playing possum." But this does not apply when said possum is on fire. The burning marsupial began to twitch and eventually woke up to the realization that—well—it was on fire. This did not sit well with the possum, and it began to growl and chase after the screaming boys, who were thoroughly shocked that their little joke had turned into actual animal cruelty. As the possum chased the boys around the yard, an adult emerged from the house with a gun and ended the escapade. He was not happy about what he had just witnessed.

Now it was almost time for the party to start, and the boys had a decision to make.

Choose Your Own Adventure

▶ **A:** If you want to toss the possum in the swimming pool turn to page 120.

▶ **B:** If you want to replace one of the pizzas in a pizza box with the possum turn to page 121.

I often use this story as an intro to my sermon on going from death to life or being on fire for Christ—but either way, it's a stretch. I just love to see delight (and disgust) in people's eyes. Laughter is important.

What if we were actually meant to enjoy God, his people, and his creation? What if our primary purpose did resemble the assertion of the Westminster Shorter Catechism, "to glorify God and enjoy him forever"? A dodgeball theology refuses to equate holiness with some kind of mundane, rule-keeping, obligatory religion but rather suggests that new life in Christ brings a certain level of wonder, awe, vibrancy, joy. A childlike faith can spur us on to maturity, a place where we playfully decide to go on to the deeper things of God. If our churches and ministries were as joyful as they should be, there would be obvious hilarity about gathering together. We would be joyful. We would play. We would laugh.

Berryman says,

There is always a connection between pleasure and true play… The deep pleasure of godly play comes from the mastery and growth that take place within our human limits by means of our relationship with God, the creator. This relationship helps us discover our deep identity as creatures who create. This discovery in turn enables us to cope by creating with and transcending the existential limits that both confine and help define us.[50]

If our relationship with Christ, our die-to-our-self-live-in-him baptism, does not give birth to new and deeper identity in our lives, we will never really experience the abundant life God has called us to. Too often we find ministries that are so serious about the mission they've forgotten to enjoy the journey.

This is not a call to naïvely dismiss the importance of the Christian mission, nor is it a call to seek comfort in the face of suffering

CHAPTER 8

and injustice. The realization of our identity in Christ will propel us headfirst into our mission of sharing hope and righting wrongs. But, as Mike Yaconelli says, "Jesus understood he could protect the seriousness of the gospel by interspersing his life and message with a sense of playfulness."[51] There is no question that our mission is serious, but we should not be so driven that we can't rest in our calling and enjoy the work and the play we've been called to. "Just because we believe the gospel is a life-and-death matter doesn't mean we have to act as if we're dead."[52]

There was once an ancient monastery filled with devoted, celibate monks who had taken all the vows devoted monks take. The task of the monks—what they did all year long—was to copy by hand all of the old books and scrolls. After years of doing this, they had copied all the originals, so they began simply to copy the copies. It was tedious work. Father Florian was the monk in charge, and a new monk asked him, "Father Florian?"

"Yes, my brother."

"Is there any chance that copying the copies of these old books might lead us to an error?"

"What kind of error?"

"Well, couldn't someone misspell a word or something? Do we ever check these copies against the originals?"

Father Florian paused and thought this new monk had a really good point. So he went down to the vault, where all the original scrolls and books were kept, and began the tedious task of comparing the latest copies with the originals. When he didn't come back, the other monks went looking for him and found him weeping uncontrollably with the scroll of vows opened on his lap.

"Father Florian, what's the problem?"

"I've found a mistake. The word was supposed to be celebrate."

This story probably never happened, but the point is, we often forsake joy for obligation. We forget that our response to God's good news is a cause for celebration. It is joy in the truest sense of the word. It is joy for us and joy for others.

Paul speaks of this joy in his letter written to the Philippians: "Rejoice in the Lord always. I will say it again: Rejoice!"[53]

One of the things we need most in our ministries and as followers of Christ is to have intelligible, responsible, historically credible, scripturally based, and life-changing thoughts about God. This is exactly what theology is. It is how and what we think about God. And spiritual theology grounds these thoughts into Trinitarian, relationship-oriented, practically applied categories. The storytellers of Scripture had intelligible and life-changing thoughts about God. This means a lot of things, but there are three things we need to pay attention to.

First, God has always been, is still, and will continue to be in the world. God is at work in the world before us, with us, and beyond us. Second, God was, is, and will be experienced by people in the world. This reality calls for us to maintain the radical optimism of the grace of God. Even today, we believe that an experience with God can change the human heart and bring life in the midst of death, light in the midst of darkness, and hope in the midst of despair. Third, it remains true that people act in certain ways because of their experiences with God.

While first about being, the Christian experience soon turns to doing. We do things a certain way to make our experience deeper, stronger, better, and more real, as well as to describe to others how this experience is possible. So the Christian does things like: follow Christ's teachings, read and memorize Scripture, pray and fast, participate in sacraments like baptism and communion, give alms, work for peace and justice, live and die well, and rejoice and celebrate. Kenda

CHAPTER 8

Dean bases much of her youth ministry model on these things that we Christians do. She calls them practices of faith and urges youth ministries to return to them.

All of these practices are important. None are to be neglected. And the spirit of celebration should take its rightful place. This was the very spirit of the angelic message ringing out through the night skies on the first Christmas: *Do not be afraid; we bring good news of great joy for everyone.* God has come into our world. You can see the mystery for yourself. And it will change you and charge you to do things differently. You need not practice these things out of obligation but with celebration and joy. To paraphrase, it's the message of Paul: *Rejoice in the Lord. You know what? In case you didn't hear it the first time, I'll say it again. Rejoice! Don't argue and worry all the time. Pray and rejoice. Be kind and love and live.*

What makes this passage even more amazing is that we find out, kind of by accident, that Paul is actually writing this letter from prison and awaiting news on a trial that could result in his death. He is also concerned that being locked up will keep him from making sure people are teaching the right things about Jesus. So here he sits, unjustly accused, in jail with no rights, in chains feeling trapped, stressed out, and he uses the opportunity to write things like: *Don't be anxious, pray, be kind, and rejoice!*

Paul has read the scrolls. He is familiar with Zephaniah and Isaiah and knows that the God who keeps his promises (even when his people don't) is a God who gives us joy in the midst of sorrow. Joy even when we're in captivity. Joy in the midst of pain.

Martin Luther comments on the Philippians passage:

> Such is the rejoicing, mark you, of which Paul here speaks—a rejoicing where there is no sin, no fear of death or hell, but rather a glad and all-powerful confidence in God and his kindness. Hence

the expression, "Rejoice in the Lord;" not rejoice in silver or gold, not in eating or drinking, not in pleasure or mechanical chanting, not in strength or health, not in skill or wisdom, not in power or honor, not in friendship or favor, nay, not in good works or holiness even. For these are deceptive joys, false joys, which never stir the depths of the heart. They are never even felt. When they are present we may well say the individual rejoices superficially, and without a heart experience.[54]

The kind of rejoicing we desire comes from a complete confidence in God. Thus, it could be said that authentic faith produces real joy.

While I think the lines are a bit blurry, there seems to be a difference between the concept of joy and the concept of happiness. I remember a counseling session I had with a man in our ministry who had decided to leave his wife. He exclaimed, "It doesn't make any sense. If the Bible and the Constitution tell me I have a God-given right to be happy, then why can't I choose to do the things in life that will make me happy?"

The pastor and history teacher came out in me, so I corrected him. "First, it wasn't the Constitution; it was the Declaration of Independence, and it simply states that we have the right to *pursue happiness*, but it says nothing about perpetual happiness. And Scripture talks more about humility, submission, and the *joy* that comes from being in right relationship with God rather than as a God-given right; for *joy* can be had both in sorrow and rejoicing. It's a mystery and a gift from God; not a right." He chose his own path, which was filled with pain.

The two concepts can get confusing. The definitions are very similar. The main difference I've found is that joy is a state of being, and happiness is response to good fortune. Our goal is not to determine which word is right but to determine which action is right. Paul talks in Philippians about lasting joy. This is something more than just a happy feeling of good fortune (remember, his fortunes aren't so good). Paul later calls this same joy by the name contentment. The students in our ministries and the people in our churches may not be overly fortunate or externally happy, but a dodgeball theology asserts that, despite these things, they can be joyful.

George Bernard Shaw was a Nobel Prize-winning playwright from Ireland. In the preface of his book *Man and Superman: A Comedy and a Philosophy,* he contemplates the hero of John Bunyan's classic allegory, *Pilgrim's Progress*. With Christians in mind he writes:

> This is the true joy in life, the being used for a purpose recognized by yourself as a mighty one: the being thoroughly worn out before you are thrown on the scrap heap, and being a force of nature instead of a feverish selfish little clod of ailments and grievances, complaining that the world will not devote itself to making you happy.[55]

Being used for a mighty purpose is important in cultivating a joyful life. Purpose is essential for our young people today. How are our ministries creating positive paths to purpose for children and adolescents? One beautiful thing about the Christian way is its inherent calling for followers to imagine themselves as part of the grand purpose of joining with Christ in his rescue of the world.[56] Our ministries offer joy as they offer purpose.

Shaw's idea of "being thoroughly worn out" toward this idea of purpose is interesting to consider. As Bunyan's pilgrims experience the long, hard road, so we who walk the path of Christ know what it is to be exhausted and used up for the sake of others. Our *Nephesh* is depleted because it is exhausting to be a creative force in the world. This is why we need pauses and times of Sabbath replenishment. And this is an equation for joy. The final observation from Shaw's statement on joy is the idea of being a force of nature as opposed to a "selfish little clod of ailments and grievances." When we are certain of our identity as creatures made in the image of the Creator, we can find a rhythm in life that is true to our nature. When we do this, we avoid the kind of life-draining activities that cause us to be self-serving and miserable.

Joy, laughter, and authentic play are needed in our ministries today. The question is, how do we cultivate joy and laughter into the lives of other people? How can people who seem so miserable be enticed to laugh and play? In Matthew 11:28-30 we hear the calling of a playful Christ: "Come to me, all you who are weary and burdened, and I will give you rest. Take my yoke upon you and learn from me, for I am gentle and humble in heart, and you will find rest for your souls. For my yoke is easy and my burden is light."

Charles Swindoll, in his book *Laugh Again,* claims that this passage contains what he calls the hidden secret to a happy life. He writes:

Did you catch the key words? "I am gentle and humble in heart," which might be summed up in the one word *unselfish.* According to Jesus' testimony, that is the most Christlike attitude we can demonstrate. Because he was so humble—so unselfish—the last person he thought of was himself. To be "humble in heart" is to be submissive to the core. It involves being more interested in serving the needs of others than in having one's own needs met.[57]

He goes on:

In our selfish, grab-all-you-can-get society, the concept of cultivating an unselfish, servant-hearted attitude is almost a joke to the majority. But, happily, there are a few (I hope you are one of them) who genuinely desire to develop such an attitude. I can assure you, if you carry out that desire, you will begin to laugh again—and I mean really laugh. It is the hidden secret of a happy life.[58]

Though Swindoll uses the word *happy* (like I said, the line is blurry) the point is not lost on us. Joy stems from unselfishness. Selfishness is another of those things that takes the life out of our souls.

A dodgeball theology is simply a developed theology of joy, play, and laughter. It calls us to cultivate a curriculum that continues to teach a message of submission, serving, and unselfish giving. When we can temper our seemingly insatiable need to be recognized or promoted above others, when we can follow the example of a Christ who was gentle and humble, we can experience an amazing outpouring of joy with the inevitable outcome of laughter and play, regardless of our circumstances. Karl Barth calls Paul's joy a defiant, nevertheless, *I will have joy* attitude.

It strikes me that, as Paul writes this letter to the Philippians, he thinks about the issues with the church. In fact, he even names names. He says Eudoia and Synsynthe should stop their arguing! When I tried to find these two women's names anywhere else in Scripture, I came up empty. It hit me. How would I like it if I was known for my arguing spirit? This wouldn't sit well with me. I want to celebrate. I want to experience the kindness and joy of Christ. I want to laugh.

Laughter has not been a serious subject for most systematic theologians. Laughter has been looked at suspiciously throughout the history of the Christian church. Thinkers have debated issues about Christ and his humanity and whether laughter had any place in his life or whether it should have any place in the lives of his followers.

Berryman says,

In general, large organizations, including the church, do not tolerate laughter very well, but in the church laughter has always remained alive somewhere. Where there is laughter there is also play, and where there is play there is the possibility of the godly game.[59]

We are being called by the kindness of Christ to engage in a godly kind of play that will bring moments of joy and laughter into our lives.

CHAPTER 9

THE DANCE

> Trinity keeps pulling us into a far larger world
> than we can imagine on our own.
> —Eugene Peterson[60]

I took my three daughters to a daddy-daughter ball here in our hometown. We walked out on the dance floor and all four danced together. It wasn't necessarily graceful or overly rhythmic, but it was meaningful. It didn't last long, though, because my six-year-old wanted to do knee slides and breakdance moves, my ten-year-old wanted to kick it with her friends, and my thirteen-year-old was a little embarrassed to be seen with her dad in public. But, at least for that one dance, we were all together.

What if God functioned as dance more than anything else? What if God was a relationship with fluid and graceful movements? Maybe he is.

CHAPTER 9

I walked out of my first theology class in seminary, went directly to the bookstore, and bought a small book that had definitions for theological terms. It was like I purchased a tourist translation book. This was a language all its own, and my undergrad education courses didn't use these words. My head was buried in that book most of the semester. I often heard a word and had to read the definition three times before I could even think about understanding it. And the upperclassmen seemed to relish using all those words!

One day, one of my classmates raised his hand and said something like, "Dr. R, I was astounded last night in my exegesis by the implications of my presuppositions toward the Trinitarian doctrine as the Greek term *perichoresis* indicates by the differentiation attained by the unique personalities of the Trinity while maintaining these personalities, which indeed remain unique as well as healthily enmeshed." At this point my brain exploded. The only term I could remember with what I had left was the word *perichoresis* in the middle of the sentence. When I read the definition of the term, I found it to be a beautiful concept, even if I didn't fully understand it.

Theologians have agreed that this term is a way of describing the mutual yet specific and unique interactions of the different entities of the Trinity. The term is actually the Greek word for dance. Peterson claims the ancient Greeks used the term as a metaphor for the Trinity.

Imagine a folk dance, a round dance, with three partners in each set. The music starts up and the partners holding hands begin to move in a circle. On signal from the caller, they release hands, change partners, and weave in and out, swinging first one and then another. The tempo increases, the partners move more swiftly with and between and among one another, swinging and twirling, embracing and releasing, holding on and letting go. But there is no confusion, every movement is cleanly coordinated in precise rhythms (these are practiced and skillful dancers!), as each person maintains his or her identity.[61]

The Trinity as a theology was developed early in the history of the church, and when you think about it, it really is a beautiful description of just how Christ is related to God and Spirit.

If we claim God is essentially relationship by nature, than the development of a robust theology of play seems natural. If we hold on to the Trinitarian concept of God, then we can progress to a common understanding of a God who works and plays, creates and rests, reconciles and reconstructs, tears down and builds up—and all these things together as a trio of completely unique but completely connected beings.

James and Judith Balswick claim that this Trinitarian understanding of God also speaks to the kind of relationship families and marriage partners should have with one another and that communities might have together.

Like a round dance, marriage can be described as two people moving rhythmically together as they repeatedly embrace, release, hold on, and then let go of each other . . . It may be an ever-changing dance with new moves as circumstances alter, but when spouses are in step there is great joy in observing the graceful movements.[62]

It follows that if this *perichoresis* concept can be applied not only to the interaction of God but the interaction of spouses in relationship, then it could be taken a step further to describe the personal relationship between a person and God as well as the relationships of the Christian community.

The authors discuss the contribution of theologian Miroslav Volf, who translated this Trinitarian theology into a "model of the church as a Christian community."[63] The key sticking point is the idea that, just like the persons of the Trinity, the Christian community both maintains the unique quality of the individual but does so in the context of how the individual relates with others and with God. We are independent and at the same time interdependent. We are individuals but function together as a connected whole.

This whole concept of Trinity and the dance of God can inform our theology as well as our practice. Good thoughts about God should equally lead to good actions. Theology is a spiritual thing, but spirituality is about persons, and persons are about being in relationship, and being begets doing. Peterson says it this way.

> Without an adequately imagined theology, spirituality gets reduced to the cramped world reported by journalists or the flat world studied by scientists. Trinity reveals the immense world of God creating, saving, and blessing in the name of Father, Son, and Holy Spirit with immediate and lived implications for the way we live, for our spirituality. Trinity is the church's attempt to understand God's revelation of Godself in all its parts and relationships. And a most useful work it has been. At a most practical level it provides a way of understanding and responding to the God who enters into all the day-to-day issues that we face as persons and churches and communities from the time we get out of bed in the morning until we fall asleep at night, and reaches out to bring us into participation on God's terms, that is, on Trinitarian terms. It prevents us from getting involved in highly religious but soul-destroying ways of going about living the Christian life.[64]

This is a pretty good summation of what we're after in our youth ministry. We must begin with solid, biblical-historical, "adequately imagined," thoroughly thought-out theology. This theology reveals to us the nature of a God who is holy, who transcends our senses, who is personal, who keeps promises, who creates, who restores, who weeps, laughs, rejoices, and plays. Ours is a God who dances. A God who was, is, and will be. A God in relationship. We see his glory in the Son, the one who has come to save and to show us how we should live. Ours is a God who frees us from the bondage of brick quotas and "highly religious but soul-destroying ways" of life. This freedom calls us to humbly submit all of our lives to him with no reserve. It's an ongoing submission, a daily surrender of our own rights, a progressive dance we get better at with time.

All ministry activity then arises from these things. We learn to play the godly game. We learn that we are created in his likeness. We learn that his likeness is relationship. We learn to love God as we were created to, and ourselves, and others, and this world. We strive to really live. To be committed to a real communion of believers. We learn to look for and savor moments. We learn to confess, be honest, and be blessed by the forgiveness of others. Our youth ministries and churches remain dynamic, unpredictable, fluid, and alive, on fire with joy and celebration.

We enter into a new kind of time. We find a place where heaven and earth intersect, a place where we are brought face to face with the Christ who defeated the seriousness of the cross with the playfulness of the empty tomb. We learn to play together for the good of the world. And we have a decision to make.

Choose Your Own Adventure

- ▶ **A:** If you want to see what dodgeball theology looks like in youth ministry go to page 85.
- ▶ **B:** If you don't, then close this book, get up, go forth, and play!

SECTION TWO

PRACTICAL PLAY IN YOUTH MINISTRY

There have been areas, programs, and approaches in my ministries over the years that I wouldn't recommend to anyone. Sometimes my own programming has been inefficient, archaic, and just plain lame. I've made mistakes. Sometimes I even learned from them. There are so many youth pastors who do so many things well. We all have our strengths and weaknesses, I suppose.

What I would like to offer is tangible evidence of how a dodgeball theology has fostered Christian growth and magical moments in youth ministry for more than two decades. I realize that success is difficult to define in ministry. I once felt I was successful in ministry when I grew wide (numbers) with little concern for depth (Christian growth). Now I realize my ministry philosophy was just fat and shallow. There have been other times when success in ministry simply meant keeping my executive pastor from convincing the senior pastor to fire me.

The point is, success is subjective. It always seems to be shifting, depending on the situations we find ourselves in. Realizing success requires a careful examination of culture and the needs, deficiencies, and desires of the people we are called to minister to.

When we can define it, we will be more likely to achieve it.

CHAPTER 10

THE PERFECT PLAYER
Quest for Spiritual Maturity

> How many young people come to our events and programs is not the most important way to evaluate how our ministry is doing. Forming Christians who have godly character and a passion for Christ doesn't happen overnight. We should be thinking about where our young people will be in their life with God not only next week, but also ten or forty years from now. Cutting corners to get immediate spiritual results with our youth will rarely last.
>
> —Mike King[65]

One of the first things we need to do is paint a picture of what we want our students (and adults) to look like in the end. Borrowing from Stephen Covey, we want to "begin with the end in mind." Too often our ministries, despite their well-worded purpose statements, do not have well-developed visions of what Christian maturity looks like.

CHAPTER 10

This may be one compelling reason I have stayed passionate in youth ministry as long as I have. We see students not as they are but as they could be. The great thing about working with teenagers is that often there is still room in their lives for movement toward that end. When you come to the place where you fail to see the godly potential of the students you pastor, it's time to heed the advice of Ben (Obi-Wan) Kenobi in *Star Wars* and simply . . . move along. Dean says, "Only a playful God can re-create us, accepting our participation as we are but also presenting us in a larger vision of who we could become."[66]

Teenagers have both arrived and not yet arrived. They are transitioning into their own faith, finding their own voice, but they are not yet all they ought to be. While this is true of all of us, it is radically true for adolescents. I suppose this is because they are still exponentially more flexible, moldable, and open to change than most adults.

It's important to verbalize the vision we have for our students. They need to hear we believe in them, but they also need to know we expect a lot from them. In the book *Passing on the Faith,* Merton Strommen and Richard Hardel suggest some valuable things that we have or have tried to implement over the years. Their primary assertion suggests faith development is dependent primarily on parents, who are first-tier influencers in the lives of their kids. Any kind of youth ministry that does not recognize the essential influence of parents on the faith lives of kids will never be effective in passing faith on. This does not mean that all parents will do a good job at this, but it does mean we pastors take seriously the religious education of parents from our youth ministries. The authors have also identified important characteristics that mark the life of a mature or committed Christian. This is beginning with the end in mind.

At the risk of digressing, I would like to offer this idea as paramount to a Wesleyan-Arminian youth ministry approach. What I have concluded after numerous debates and discussions with my reformed friends is that we don't necessarily differ that much in our definitions of mature Christian commitment, but we do approach the teaching act and the process differently.

Rarely do I emphasize to my students that they just need to accept their inadequacies, sins, failures, and mistakes as essential parts of their imperfect humanity. As true as it might be and as much moral relief as it might offer, I would rather choose to hold in front of them the idealistic expectations of Christ, who calls us to attain some level of perfection.

Admittedly, there is a balancing act that takes place here. We must offer students assurances of their salvation but at the same time remind them of the need to go further down the road toward the mature life. Instead of calling the goal of perfect love impossible, we should keep it before our students as a challenge to be greater, through the sanctifying work of Christ, than they ever imagined. This is imaginative youth ministry.

Recently I met with the parents in my ministry and began to discuss these characteristics of a committed Christian and what we want to see in their students. Our characteristics are our own variations of Strommen and Hardel's list.[67]

We want committed youth who:

1) Trust in Christ. They actually know and trust in Jesus.
2) Get God's grace. They live in grace and offer grace and forgiveness to others.
3) Connect with God. They take time for silence, prayer, and Scripture reading in a consistent attempt to commune with God.

4) Do right things. They demonstrate Christian morality and right actions.

5) Commit to the congregation. They stay involved in a local church even after leaving high school.

6) Actively love others. They show genuine compassion and concern for other people.

7) Are hopeful, positive, and joyful. They know how to laugh, play, and live into the radical optimism of God's grace.

8) Do Christian things. They participate in rituals and practices of the Christian community.

9) Are compassionate. They work to help people who are in need and lead them to wholeness.

This seems simple enough, but a thoroughly established vision of maturity is often lacking in youth ministry. Constructing this vision of the Christian individual is important in the development of a corporate youth ministry philosophy. We know what our ministries should look like, but what about the students involved in our ministries? This idea, though often unspoken, has been an important motivator to me in developing imaginative youth ministry.

What becomes clear when we consider these marks of maturity is an understanding that, though this looks like a destination, it is more like a direction. We walk together on the pathway of maturity. We begin to get familiar with the way. We learn the steps we need to take. Our feet form to the path, and the path becomes worn by our travel.

This is the path we walk with our students. It is a playful path filled with rest stops, roadside parks, and historical markers. We walk there together. Sometimes we lead. Sometimes we follow. All the while, we watch and wait for things that can teach us, encourage us, and motivate us to keep walking.

CHAPTER 11

HOOKED ON LITURGY
Creative Worship

> The most valuable thing the Psalms do for me is to express
> that same delight in God which made David dance.
> —C. S. Lewis[68]

There were fifteen kids in an old church van who agreed to go with me to a concert by a new group that primarily focused on worship music. This wasn't normal in those days. Few bands were making it in the industry with sing-along worship music. Sonic Flood was an exception. The specific denomination and the local church I grew up in was not an overly emotional or expressive bunch (unless we were all in heat-induced worship hypnosis at summer camp meetings). Something happened at that Sonic Flood concert that opened my eyes to new possibilities in worship.

It was a controlled freedom, a calm openness, and an authentic expression of deep love in restrained but emotional ways. As they sang and praised, my typically reserved, quiet, and unexpressive students lifted hands, knelt, sat in silence, stood in reverence, cried, prayed, hugged, and, well, worshiped. It was a beautiful thing.

CHAPTER 11

That was a formative moment for me as I saw these typically non-expressive, postmodern student leaders drawn into authentic, corporate, two-way conversations with God in passionate and real ways. God used this moment to change me and plant a vision in me for a new kind of worship ministry. From that moment on, we have playfully and creatively approached worship in our youth ministry, and often it has challenged our church to consider new paradigms.

To approach worship with imagination is challenging, given the diverse cultural climate in the church today. This is especially true if we make serious attempts to include youth and their interests in the design of worship ministries for the entire congregation, as opposed to a segregated sub-group. The difficulties arise with the evident language and cultural gap in the traditional church. There are, in every church with multiple generations, no fewer than two different languages being spoken at any given time, and neither of these languages, though both are English, is being translated well by the different cultures. As has been well documented, there is a major cultural shift occurring in the world and in the church, and we are just beginning to see the consequences.

The rapid increases in technology alone are mind-boggling for the average adult. As we drove in a church van to Florida last summer, several of the teen girls sat behind me, playing Catch Phrase. This electronic gadget shows a word and starts a timer. The object of the game is to get your teammates to guess the word without doing motions or saying any form of the word. One of the girls looked at a word and said, "Okay. It's a form of communication. And it's really old-fashioned."

In less than a second the other girl shouted, "Email!"

"Correct." <Click>, and she passed it along.

Amazing. I just laughed, knowing many of my own peers, much less my parents' generation, have just gotten used to using email. We youth pastors, out of necessity, have become literate in these new forms of communication. So perhaps we are called to become cultural translators because a vast majority of the congregation does not thoroughly understand the degrees to which the world has changed.

Adolescents simply process information in completely different ways from how their parents and grandparents did. They think differently. I realize this subject of culture shift and modern versus postmodern culture is being worn out in multiple circles. However, when examining worship in the church and the differences between the generations, it's difficult to avoid. The church must be aware of these differences. It must become fluent in these languages. It must somehow find balances and validate both and/or all of the cultural groups it's composed of.

It used to be that ski lodges banned snowboarders from their slopes. To open their mountain to these punk kids and their skateboards without wheels would surely result in a lower class of clientele with more injuries and more fights. The purist was one who gently carved the snow with skis, not one who sought out every jump, rail, stump, and log on the hill and descended straight down with no carve or grace. The two cultures couldn't exist together.

It was 1983 when the first major ski operation allowed snowboarders legal access to their mountain. The raging success prompted other slopes to follow suit but not because they wanted to; just because it was big business. Today, there are only three ski slopes in America that don't allow snowboarding. The cultures have merged, even if there is still some level of angst between the two.

This is similar to what is happening in the church today. We have (at least) two vastly different cultures at the same place for similar reasons with completely different methods and mentalities dictating how the experience should occur. Both groups love the essential foundations that compose the experience. The steep hills, new powder, tree runs, and chair lifts on the slope are replaced with things like authentic experience of God, answers to life's toughest questions, the peace of Christ, and a life of purposeful fulfillment found in him. These are things both groups still long for; they just get to them in different ways. To open up the church to both cultures is challenging but not impossible.

In 1998, after my personal sonic flood in worship, I began to imagine what a church that spoke both of these cultural languages would look like. I was the youth pastor in a mid-size church of about five hundred folks. My imagination was much larger than just offering new styles of music. This, however, was the most public, observable issue that needed to be addressed. As a youth pastor, I knew my influence was limited, but I was convinced (and still am) that if our visions for the church flow from an authentic, humble, positive, and passionate heart, there is hope for them.[69] My imagination led me to discuss the idea with the senior pastor of the church, and we began a new service on Saturday nights.

This passion and vision stayed with me and was reconfirmed several times over in every church I have served since. The vision is not segregation. If we wanted a completely separate, youth-driven worship experience, we could do that in our own youth ministry bubbles. We decided that this vision was to be for the whole mountain, the whole church.

We soon discovered that the style, methods, and languages were so vastly different that finding a common language in one setting was difficult. In 2001 we attended a youth ministry conference, and I used it more as a vacation than anything else. I attended only one seminar led by a Vanilla-Ice-looking pastor from California whom I had never heard of named Dan Kimball. He challenged us to be bold enough to plant new services in our churches. I remember someone asking the question, "What about the loss of intergenerational community?"

He responded with something like, "We don't dare jeopardize this in the church. The church is best with multiple generations caring for each other. However, do you see authentic community taking place in a one-hour service where the people rarely even talk to each other, much less really get to know each other? Do you see koinonia taking place with a thirty-second handshake to the person who happened to sit by you that day? Community in the church takes place outside these services as people really get to know one another. This idea that our current, entertainment-driven, congregational model of worship is the only right way to do things is misinformed."

This stuck with me. As a church leader I wanted to open the whole mountain up to the different cultures, languages, methods, and desires. And we wanted to do this with a ski slope that was already filled with both cultures. So we have continued to plant new services and build community in common connections outside those services.

This multi-service, congregation-within-congregation approach may not work or be palatable for everyone, but over the years, we've seen some amazing things happen. At the church where I currently serve, our pastoral staff began to play with these ideas. We started this service with the desire to reach new people for Christ and then moved it from Tuesday to Sunday night then eventually added it as a second service. We were becoming culturally bilingual.

We then started another bilingual service and ministry with the desire to reach new people for Christ. This one was targeted toward people who actually spoke a different language (Spanish). So we now offer three entirely different services with three unique congregations who are encouraged to connect with each other on a regular basis. We are a trilingual church with multiple cultures and generations under one roof in one accord.

We choose not to talk about young and old, contemporary or traditional, and modern or postmodern. We simply offer multiple services for multiple groups. We have different pastors, who speak the language of the congregation, preaching at each of these services. We've seen growth in so many ways. And we have a blast!

The vision that was birthed in me at that concert and reaffirmed over the years has become a living, breathing reality. What a joy! It's so much fun being able to form and fashion worship that is meaningful for people. Worship has become a type of play. It's challenging to figure out new ways to experience Scripture. It's exciting to reinstate some ancient practices that have long since been removed from our evangelical circles.

Here are just some elements in the worship service I lead:

| **Low lights and lit candles.** | This element has, much to my surprise, been the number-one source of concern from church members who do not attend this service. *Have we gone Catholic? Are you guys having a séance in there? What's with all the darkness and candles?* I explain that candles have been lit in Christian worship from the beginning. We light candles to provide what many in our generation believe to be a sacred, reflective environment. We light candles to symbolize our prayers. As smoke rises to the sky, so our prayers go to God. Low lights make the candles shine in the darkness. They also allow people to totally focus on worship. |

Fourfold pattern of worship.	In every service for seven years, we've put four words on the screens indicating our movement from one segment of the worship service to the other. We *GATHER* with celebratory songs, welcome, and greeting. We the church, though scattered across the world throughout the week, gather once again to worship. We *PROCLAIM* the good news of Christ by reading Lectionary scriptures, singing songs of proclamation, saying creeds together, and preaching from Scripture. We *RESPOND* to the message we've heard by prayer, participation, communion, candle lighting, or silent commitment. We are then *SENT* into the world through charge and benediction. It's not new for many mainline denominations, but it's been fun to bring it to life in our setting.
Extended greeting time and passing the peace of Christ.	We take about five minutes (which seems like an eternity sometimes) to talk to people and connect; to get up and move around and meet new people and really connect. We also pass the peace of Christ. *May the peace of Christ be with you. And also with you.*
New music and old hymns done in new ways.	Several of the older people in the congregation love the fact that we sing hymns on a regular basis. The music certainly sounds new, with a band and worship leaders, but we value meaningful songs, new or old.

Video as iconography.	Many attenders are comfortable with complex images. They respond to image. Their minds can handle fast-moving images layered on top of one another. Our media is a ministry. It is a vehicle of worship that we take seriously. Our words are always layered on images.
Attention to Lectionary and church year.	We have found so much enjoyment from following the Lectionary. We aren't bound by it. We diverge and probably break a lot of liturgical "rules." But so what? It's been a blessing to incorporate recognitions of days like Trinity Sunday and Ash Wednesday into our services.
Participatory and creative responses.	We challenge our people to respond each week, but often we try to get creative. We've used many different kinds of prayer stations. We connect our responses to the proclamation. Besides the altar, communion, and candles, we've used Legos, Jenga blocks, clay pots, poker chips, dirt, water, glass, the Game of Life, trophies, etc. . . . I am always looking for new ways to challenge people to participate and respond.
Creeds and responsive readings.	We say the Lord's Prayer, the Apostles' Creed, the Nicene Creed, and read responsively various prayers and laments from Scripture. This is a meaningful way to draw people to participate.
Regular communion.	We take communion no less than once a month. We've tinkered with the idea of offering every week. We find it to be the most meaningful responsive expression of the ongoing Christian life.

No special music or performances.	We de-emphasize performance from the stage or pulpit. We don't encourage or desire applause. We want to focus on our corporate worship of God, and we choose not to focus on the talents of men and women.
Freedom for movement and expression.	We don't coerce people to respond. We never ask them to stand up, but we allow them to. We offer the altar as a good place to pray, but we don't beg for response. We want people to make intelligible decisions for Christ without manipulation.

These are some of the ways we play in worship. This service has become a meaningful part of my own Christian expression. Our church has responded well to the differences. We are still one church. We connect at different levels. We are filled with young and old. We celebrate victories together. We are growing in more ways than one. And we are constantly imagining, being creative, and playing together.

CHAPTER 12

PLAYFUL DEVOTION
A Table for Two

> The last barrier to full intimacy with the Savior is hurriedness. Intimacy may not be rushed. To meet with the Son of God takes time. We have learned all too well the witless art of living fast. We gulp our meals sandwiched between pressing obligations. The table of communion with the inner Christ is not a fast-food franchise.
> —Calvin Miller[70]

One Sunday, I began my sermon in front of a table with two chairs, two plates, two mugs, and a pitcher filled with freshly brewed coffee. It made the sanctuary smell wonderful. When it was time for me to speak, I simply walked up to the table and sat down alone. Without saying a word, I poured myself a cup of steaming coffee and started to drink it. I got my phone out and began to mess with it, still saying nothing. The silence became uncomfortable.

CHAPTER 12

When everyone started to fidget, a teenager named Kara got up, walked down the aisle, and sat in the empty chair. I looked at her and said, "You want some coffee?"

"Sure," she replied.

I poured, and we both drank and just started talking. "How was your week?"

"Fine, boring. I got an A on my chemistry test."

"Wow. That's impressive. Were your parents proud?"

"Uh, sure, I guess. We really didn't talk about it much. They wouldn't expect anything different."

We chatted a bit about her week, her life, nothing big, just what was going on. Then I said to her, "Kara, you know I think you're incredible! Please keep living the way you're living. Keep playing. Keep having fun. Keep smiling and loving others. Hope to see you soon."

"Uh . . . Okay, sure. Thanks for the coffee," she said as she got up and went back to her seat.

I had been talking about finding and following a path to disciplined Christian living. The goal of a ministry infused with imagination and play, a dodgeball theology, is not to be frivolous but to be mature in our Christian faith. It is not to be tossed back and forth in our faith. It is to continue on a path of disciplined living. This means we all should be doing several things with our lives.

We should grow up and begin to see the world differently. We should find a steady pace, knowing this journey is not a sprint but a lifelong endurance race that requires us to begin with the end in mind. It means we should discipline the body and refrain from loose living and gluttony to better serve the kingdom of God. It means we will use our brains and become thinkers, not merely reactors. A disciplined life means we will count it a blessing when we face trials and thrive in the interruptions of life. It means we will refuse to live by feelings and impulses but will do the right thing with self-control. It also means we will learn that there are seasons in life, rhythms and timings that must be learned and respected. We must learn the art of waiting.

Dodgeball theology means we encourage our students to discipline their lives not out of obligation but because they passionately desire to be used by God in his kingdom. We must encourage our students and leaders to practice their faith and "cultivate patterns of prayer."[71]

The apostle Peter speaks of people patterning their lives after Christ, becoming disciplined, and refraining from immoral and unhealthy things so accepted in the world.

He reminds everyone that we will have to give an account of our lives in the end, which brings to surface the question of how we should live our lives. I heard about a man who, instead of asking, "What do you do for a living?" when he meets people, asks, "What in your life have you done that you're proud of?" I want to live my life in such a way that I'm proud of the things I've done. To do this I must heed the words of 1 Peter 4:7-11:

> The end of all things is near. Therefore be alert and of sober mind so that you may pray. Above all, love each other deeply, because love covers over a multitude of sins. Offer hospitality to one another without grumbling. Each of you should use whatever gift you have received to serve others, as faithful stewards of God's grace in its various forms. If anyone speaks, they should do so as one who speaks the very words of God. If anyone serves, they should do so with the strength God provides, so that in all things God may be praised through Jesus Christ. To him be the glory and the power for ever and ever. Amen.

CHAPTER 12

I believe the key to any good theology is the practice of it. Thoughts of God must be measured by real-life experience with God and how those thoughts apply to the real world. To know God means more than knowledge in the formal theological, academic sense. To know God means we commune with him. It means we practice—and encourage the people we influence to practice—positive patterns of prayer.

Calvin Miller describes our time with Christ as dining with Christ at a table in the wilderness.

"Fellowship with Christ is a table only for two—set in the wilderness. Inwardness is not a gaudy party, but the meeting of lovers in the lonely desert of the human heart. There, where all life and fellowship can hold no more than two, we sit together and he speaks as much as we, and even when both of us say nothing there is our welded oneness. And suddenly we see we cannot be complete until his perfect presence joins with ours."[72]

It's a specific time and place where we enlist our lives into the life of Christ, our play into the play of Christ.

Kara meeting me at the table at the beginning of my sermon was a playful illustration of prayer. I waited for Kara to come to the table for two. (Of course, I called her ahead of time.) I guess she trusted me enough to do it. So she came, and we sat and talked. I already knew she wanted her coffee black, but I let her say it out loud. What she thirsted for, she received. What she hungered for was hers. And we just talked about life. We didn't talk about systematic theology, eschatology, or any other -ology. We didn't discuss the dispensation of the Holy Spirit. Though I would have loved to talk about those things, it was more of a personal conversation, between friends, at the table for two.

Over the years, I've realized that youth ministry is good at flashy programs, high-energy outreaches, stellar mission experiences, and amazing Thursday-night-camp altar calls, but youth ministry is often deficient in the call to contemplative, deep, lasting, joyful, passionate relationship and conversation with the living Christ. We all need a table for two. God is calling and waiting for you, your students, your ministry, your church. Will you carve out time for him in your life? He knows better than anyone what we hunger for, what we need. He wants us to know him better. He'll talk about anything.

We have to take time for authentic leisure. Miller mentions the church fathers who often spoke of *otium sanctum,* or "holy leisure."[73] We can't come rushing into the presence of Christ checking our watches and expect to experience the kind of play, joy, peace, assurance, hope, and genuine leisure we need in this frantically busy world.

The *otium sanctum* is true leisure in the middle of a busy life. Most of our hurriedness is really a cover for sloth. When we cram our calendars with appointments, we may delude ourselves that we are busy. But busy about what? We are tending the whirligigs of the trivial afraid that if we stop we will see the emptiness of our lives.[74]

We need—I need—to keep encouraging people to engage with Christ at a table for two in the wilderness. This is the foundation of true joy. This is a place of play and replenishment.

Of course, knowing and practicing are vastly different. We need to carve out time in our churches and youth ministries for prayer. We need to focus on the need for real communion with Christ. And it isn't getting easier. Even if we corporately allow for silence and solitude, which is valuable on occasion, we still have teenagers who live noisy lives. How can we encourage students to take time with Christ at the table for two?

1. **Model it.** We should be able to report to others what life with Christ at the table is really like. We must let Christ nurture us. We must be replenished on a regular basis.
2. **Teach it.** This push toward inwardness should be part of our curriculum. We're good at the outward things of ministry and need to work on these formative practices.
3. **Allow for it.** We need to allow students to carve out this time. Maybe it's just one less program a month or year. Maybe it's a retreat designed around this purpose. Maybe it's part of our regular offerings.
4. **Value it.** We need to communicate with students and praise those who report strong devotional lives. Students will know what we value. We should value the deeper things of Christ.

CHAPTER 13

JOYFUL JOURNEYS
Trips as Play

> God is not only present when we can see him,
> he is present when we can't, and joy comes from
> recognizing God in places we never thought he would be.
> —Mike Yaconelli[75]

Trips and retreats are significant elements in a thoroughly developed youth ministry. All of the specific aspects important to a dodgeball theology are present and more pronounced on a trip. They become joyful journeys—sacred in very real ways. They remain etched in the memories of people forever. Students will forget your sermons and cute ideas, but they will always remember those playful times on the river, in the mission, on the mountain, in places of poverty, and in climates of prayer and dependence on God.

Earlier this year, we were packing a 5x8 trailer with our luggage, food, and equipment for the annual ski trip. A man from our congregation was there for a meeting with the 12-Step group he leads every

CHAPTER 12

Friday night at the church. When he saw us packing the trailer he came and told us about a ski trip he took with his youth group thirty-some years ago. He laughed as he recalled some of the crazy things that happened on that trek to the mountains.

He said, "My life was never as good as it was in those days. I made a mess of it with drugs and alcohol and a whole series of bad decisions. But it was moments like those that reminded me later in life of who I was and what I could be. So I'm back now, my life has been miraculously changed, I can laugh again, and God can still use me. Don't ever doubt it, Pastor, these trips are important."

It was a good reminder, and his is not an isolated story.

The number of trips I've taken and led in youth ministry would boggle the mind. There's a reason for my bald head, age spots, and forehead wrinkles. Many of these journeys have been mission oriented; some have been for discipleship, some for spiritual formation, some purely for recreation and fun. Some would be called successful. Some would be called dismal failures. All of them, without exception, have produced lifelong memories. All of them have reinforced my commitment to a theology that takes play, Sabbath, space, spiritual formation, and our service in the kingdom of God seriously. There is something joyful and sacred about these pilgrimages we have made.

The reality is, our youth ministry functions like a family. We aren't a replacement family. We are a family of families. We realize parents need to play the biggest role in the Christian education and faith forming of their kids. We need to encourage parents to realize this. But we also understand the need for adolescents to differentiate from their parents, being formed into their own unique persons. You can call for the death of youth ministries all you want, but until the nature of adolescents changes, there will always be a need for specific youth ministries. And where there is youth ministry, there are trips of all kinds.

In my mind is a mosaic of memories: Lives have been touched and changed from both givers and receivers. Buildings have been built. Homes have been painted. Kids have been cared for. Gardens have been grown. Wells have been dug. Canoes have sprung leaks. Churches have been remodeled. Puppets have performed. Teens have been puppets. Yards have been mown. Lawn mowers have been stolen. Vans have broken down. Buses have gotten stuck. Drywall has been tacked. Snakes have been handled. Pillows have been cheesed. Playgrounds have been constructed. Seventh graders have been taped to poles. Power sit-ups have been proven possible. Four wheelers have crashed. Lake ice has cracked. Legs broken. Rules broken. Windows broken. Hearts broken. Hope given. Hands lifted. Punches thrown. Peace found. Walls scaled. Walls erected. Walls removed. Life lived.

On trips I've seen clearer pictures of what the church should be like. Traditions are important.

Each year we put a framed picture of the Sole Thriver on the youth room wall, along with a paddle signed by all who attended the annual canoe trip. Each year we do many of the same things. Why? Tradition. We're in this together. We belong to one another. This is just what we do. Who we are. Regardless of the pain and sin in the world around us, we will hold on to one another.

One year we got up on the second day of our trip and loaded our canoes. As we turned the bend in the river, we couldn't believe our eyes. We could see at least a thousand canoes and hundreds of rafts. The river was covered completely with boats, and each of these boats contained people who had obviously been drinking beer since sunup, in contraptions I didn't even know existed. They had bongs and cannons and hats. Some had floating islands of beer tied to their boats. And they weren't paddling. They weren't moving at all. We had fifteen canoes filled with church kids, and we had just paddled our way into a combination between Daytona Beach on spring break and Girls Gone Wild. And believe me, there were girls on that river who had gone wild. It was not something I particularly wanted my students to be part of.

It really began to get scary. These people were not in the right minds. They were cussing and threatening. And they were everywhere. Finally, in all the confusion, so we wouldn't lose each other, we decided to keep the girls in the canoes and have the guys jump out and physically hold on to each other and the canoes. There we were, floating our way through this maze of sin and anger, holding on to one another so as not to lose our way.

Isn't that a beautiful picture of the church? What I want to offer students is a real community that will take care of one another. When the entire world is pressing against us, when we fear we may lose our way, we need only to take hold of one another and make our way through the mess, together. Together God uses us and keeps us. He calls it his church. Peter calls us living stones that are being stacked together to form a spiritual house. Needless to say, we had an especially moving and spiritual time around the campfire that evening.

I've heard pastors claim there is danger in short-term mission trips. We might be teaching our kids that compassionate ministry is just an event. There might be a sliver of truth in this, especially if we don't encourage our youth to serve in their local churches, homes, neighborhoods, and cities. But we should be doing that. We should be encouraging our kids to serve. And we should still take short-term mission trips, even if they're in our own cities.

I've heard youth pastors claim that every trip they take is a mission-oriented service trip. "We don't do anything that isn't spiritual and service oriented. We shouldn't waste our church's resources on just fun. They can have fun and serve others at the same time." There might be a sliver of truth in this, especially if all we do is plan fun events. But we shouldn't be doing that. We should create balanced ministries. And it is spiritually acceptable to just play a little.

Play is undervalued in our churches today. Mission trips might be overvalued. A lot of money has been spent on getting people to mission trips when just sending money to address needs would have been more effective. But the reason we don't do that is students and people want to physically serve and be a part. This is a good thing, but it's not exponentially better than going on a retreat that is geared for play and fun and that draws a person closer to Christ. There is a time for everything, says Ecclesiastes. There is a time for mission work and a time for retreat. There is a time for work and a time for play. Both are important. So we should still take retreats and trips that offer opportunities for authentic play.

Every year on our annual ski trip, several of the students and adults hike up a long, steep road to get access to the backside of the mountain that offers a long, steep ride to the bottom. It's excruciatingly painful to walk with ski boots up that road. Everything in your body says, *Stop doing this, it's not worth it,* but we trek on regardless. Every year when we get to the top, after collapsing in exhaustion, we breathe in the beauty that surrounds us. It's an amazing view. Halfway down this steep, thick-powdered bowl, we stop together and pray—again, with our eyes open. We pray drinking in the surroundings and recognizing the reality of a creative God. This little trek has become a microcosm for our approach to ministry.

We recognize God as creative. He didn't make a mundane or merely functional world. He made a world of far-reaching beauty. He made one pine tree, frosted it with snow, and said, *Do it again!*

CHAPTER 12

We recognize God as Creator and ourselves as created in his image to enjoy his glory and tend to his creation. We see ourselves as present in him on the side of that mountain. We imagine that we play a role in his amazing world.

Our realization of this good God, and our imagination of our role in his plan, pushes us to enlist our story into his story, our play into his play. We enjoy life because we have learned to enjoy him.

On the mountain, in prayer, with our eyes open, we realize that Christ brings beauty and color into the world, and through him we learn to love God, others, ourselves, and the good world he created. We can in turn find a purpose, a wholeness in life.

On the mountain, like the ground all around us, time is in essence frozen, if just for a little while. And in prayer, we transcend the ordinary and replace it with the mystery and beauty of God. We pause together in these moments and recognize this place as a place where we can find the God who offers healing, rest, and peace.

The whole experience makes us alive with joy. We celebrate the otherness and oneness of God. We take our position in this cosmic daddy-son-daughter ball. And we dance.

A: As you stand there on the island, you realize you've made it. Your questions will soon be answered. Slowly, all three of you walk over to the big barn door and slide it open. It's not locked. Why would it be? There's no easy way to get to the island. (Well, I guess you could just walk to it, but it's a secret well kept.) The door is heavy, and it takes all three of you to open it up. Once inside, you realize that someone has a master plan to . . . take over the world! Okay, not really. It's just filled with random, mundane things like picnic tables that haven't been put together and umbrellas and bricks and a dead Confederate soldier hanging from the rafters . . . Okay, not really. Just the boring stuff.

B: Why wouldn't you open the barn doors? Go open the doors, for heaven's sake. You made it this far, so take the next step. Who would actually choose not to open the barn doors? Be honest—you're not a real youth pastor, are you?

A: You laugh with everyone else, but it's only out of courtesy. You think, *He may be right. What if this thing broke?* You think these things as you hastily walk toward solid (or rather, opaque) ground, though inconspicuously because you wouldn't want your fellow youth pastors to sense your fear. Once off the glass-bottom floor, you avert your eyes and make some trite comment about how the youth group girls would be freaking out right now. Then you take an aspirin and head to the elevator.

B: You laugh at the comment and then say, "Hey, what do you think would happen if all twenty of us jumped at the same time?"

They snicker and laugh. Someone says, "It says you could be, like, ten elephants on that floor, and it would hold."

"Yeah, but would it hold twenty fat pastors who jump at the same time?"

More laughs. You say, "I'm serious. Let's do it! Who's with me? I'll count it down. One . . ."

You look around and actually have convinced some others to join you.

"Two . . ." You're beginning to wonder if this was such a good idea.

"Three!" You all jump up and land at the same time, nothing happens.

You say, "I guess it would hold ten elephants."

Later, on the way down the elevator, packed in like sardines, you say, "Hey, what would happen if we all jumped at the same time in here?"

But that's a different story.

A: You decide to try to convince the strongest men to get in the canoe and paddle across. The men refuse (including you), so you grab a couple skinny but kind of crazy-like teens to send across the rapids. They gather one end of the rope as you secure the other end to a tree. Then you shove them into the raging white water, hoping they will survive and wondering if you have their medical and liability information in order. They nearly capsize, but they make it across. They secure the rope on their shore, and you start across the river, holding on to the rope. You get into the heart of the rapids and—SNAP—your weight splits the rope in twain, and you are swept down the river.

You make it to shore before you reach the ocean, and you walk back up, humiliated and trapped on the opposite shore. Now you must get high enough upstream to plunge into the rapids and let your swimming and the speed of the water push you across the river. Your body is already numb. Your lips are blue. Hypothermia must be minutes away. You take an aspirin, write a goodbye letter to your wife, and plunge into the swiftly moving water. It's only the hand of the skinny kid you sent across earlier that pulls you to safety.

B: You decide to take all the interested teens and walk up the river a ways, being sure you can convoy across the river without missing your mark at the front of the cave. One of the teens recalls a swimming technique he learned on *Man vs Wild* called barreling and suggests you all try it.

"Just dive in and start doing barrel rolls in the direction you want to go," he says.

"Okay, Bear!" You follow the students in the water.

Amazingly, their barreling works for them, but you yell out, "Do you turn to the right or the left?"

"Right!"

"My right or the right side of the river?"

"They're the same thing. RIGHT!"

You try to start rolling, but you realize that barreling works best if you haven't gained all your summer pizza pounds, so everyone makes it but you, and you end up down the river about a mile.

The next attempt contains no barreling, and you swim safely to the other shore.

**Note: We actually tried both of these methods.

CHOOSE YOUR OWN ADVENTURES

A: You decide to wait until everyone is in the pool to expose the girls to the charred possum. But the girls refuse to get in the pool, claiming it's too cold. Your plans are thwarted. The girls narrowly escape.

B: When the pizza-delivery boy pulls into the driveway, you rush out to meet him before the girls see what's going on. You made sure you ordered the deep dish. You take the pan pizza out of the box and replace it with the charred possum. During prayer, you can't even close your eyes because of the anticipation. Of course the girls are always first to the pizza (trying to instill chivalry in the boys, after all), and as they open the box, the screaming begins, and the laughter ensues.

**Note: This is the way it actually happened, so the story goes!

NOTES

1. Chesterton, G. K. *All Things Considered* (New York: John Lane, 1909), p. 96.

2. Dean, Kenda Creasy, *Practicing Passion: Youth and the Quest for a Passionate Church* (Grand Rapids, Michigan: Wm E Eerdmans, 2004), p. 198.

3. Chesterton, G. K. Orthodoxy (New York: Dodd Mead and Company, 1908), p. 52.

4. While the cassette tape has long since disappeared, I found a similar sermon here: Tony Campolo, "If I Should Wake Before I Die." http://www.csec.org/csec/sermon/campolo_3627.htm (accessed March 23, 2011).

5. Ibid.

6. Ibid.

7. Johnston, Robert. *The Christian at Play* (Grand Rapids, Michigan, W. B. Eerdmans 1983), p. 87.

8. John 1:1-5.

9. Peterson, Eugene. *Christ Plays in Ten Thousand Places: A Conversation in Spiritual Theology* (Grand Rapids, Michigan, W. B. Eerdmans, 2005), p. 85.

10. This is one of my red-line vocabulary words. Podern: the hybrid between modern and postmodern culture that exists in Western ministries today.

11. Two years after the accident I married again, and my wife and I have had sixteen joy-filled years and three beautiful daughters together.

12. Johnston, p. 4.

13. Wright, N. T. *Simply Christian* (New York: Harper Collins, 2006), p. 10.

14. Ibid, p. 11.

15. Sjogren, Steve. *Conspiracy of Kindness* (Ventura, California: Regal Books, 1993), p. 43.

16. Wright, p. 10.

17. Dean, p. 210.

18. Genesis 1:26-28.

19. Genesis 1:31.

NOTES

20. McKnight, Scot. *40 Days Living the Jesus Creed* (Brewster, Massachusetts, Paraclete Press: 2008), pp. 30-31.

21. Yaconelli, Mike. *Dangerous Wonder: The Adventure of Childlike Faith* (Colorado Springs: Navpress, 1998), p. 79.

22. Dean, Kenda, p. 210.

23. Clark, C., Dean, K., Rahn, D. *Starting Right: Thinking Theologically about Youth Ministry* (Grand Rapids, Michigan: Zondervan), p. 80.

24. Kenda Dean and Ron Foster. *The Godbearing Life* (Nashville: Upper Room Books, 1998), p. 139.

25. Peterson, p. 3.

26. Johnston, p. 4.

27. Johnston, p. 34

28. Yaconelli, p. 73.

29. Johnston, p. 143.

30. McKnight, p. 31.

31. Johnston, p. 142.

32. Dean, pp. 208-209.

33. Clark, C. *Hurt: Inside the World of Today's Teenagers* (Grand Rapids, Michigan: Baker Academic, 2004), p. 121.

34. Ibid, p. 114.

35. Huizinga, J. *Homo Ludens* (Boston, Beacon Press, 1950), p. 8.

36. Based on Johnston's summaries of Berger's work.

37. Elkind, D. *The Hurried Child* (Cambridge, MA: De Capo Press, 1981), p. 3.

38. Brueggemann, W. *Mandate to Difference* (Louisville: John Knox, 2007), p. 153.

39. Ibid, p. 152.

40. Ibid, p. 155.

41. Ibid.

42. Ibid, p. 142.

43. Ibid.

44. Ibid, p. 152.

45. Dean and Foster, p. 187.

46. Ibid, p. 187.

47. *Remember the Titans* [2000]. Script-O-Rama. Retrieved March 20, 2011, from http://www.script-o-rama.com/movie_scripts/r/remember-the-titans-script-transcript.html.

48. Berryman, Jerome, "Godly Play: An Imaginative Approach to Religious Education" (Minneapolis, Minnesota: Augsburg Press), p. 83.

49. Ibid, pp. 84-85.

50. Ibid, p 13

51. Yaconelli, p. 76.

52. Ibid, p. 78.

53. Philippians 4:4.

54. Luther, Martin. *The Sermons of Martin Luther: Volume VI: 93-112* (Grand Rapids, Michigan, Baker Book House, 1988), p. 95.

55. Shaw, G. B. *Man and Superman: A Comedy and a Philosophy* (New York: Brentano's, 1903), p. xxxi.

56. Wright, p. 11.

57. Swindoll, C. *Laugh Again* (Nashville, Thomas Nelson, 1992), p. 79.

58. Ibid, p. 80.

59. Berryman, p. 13

60. Peterson, p. 46.

61. Ibid, p. 44.

62. Balswick, J, and Balswick, J. *The Family: A Christian Perspective on the Contemporary Home* (Grand Rapids, Michigan: Baker Books, 2007), location 866 (Kindle version).

63. Ibid, location 1710.

64. Peterson, p. 44.

65. King, Mike. *Presence-Centered Youth Ministry* (Downers Grove, Illinois: Intervarsity Press, 2006), p. 179.

66. Dean, p. 210.

67. Hardel, R.A., Strommen, M.P. *Passing on the Faith: A Radical New Model for Youth and Family Ministry* (Winona, Minnesota: St. Mary's Press, 2000), p. 73.

68. Lewis, C.S. *Reflections on the Psalms* (Orlando, Harcourt Press: 1958), p. 45.

69. I would also add "divinely inspired" and "God directed," but I've seen those phrases thrown around so often by people in the church (pastors included) who are convinced that God was made in their image, so this crazy idea of theirs

must be God telling them to do it. I finally told one of the pastors I was on staff with that I found it odd how God's will was always what *he* wanted.

70. Miller, Calvin. *The Table of Inwardness* (Downers Grove, Illinois: Intervarsity Press, 1984), p. 35.

71. Taylor, R. S. *The Disciplined Life* (Kansas City: Beacon Hill Press, 1962).

72. Miller, C. *The Table of Inwardness* (Downers Grove, Illinois: Intervarsity Press, 1984), p. 22.

73. Ibid, p. 35.

74. Ibid, p. 36.

75. Yaconelli, p. 82.

www.ingramcontent.com/pod-product-compliance
Lightning Source LLC
LaVergne TN
LVHW051525070426
835507LV00023B/3306

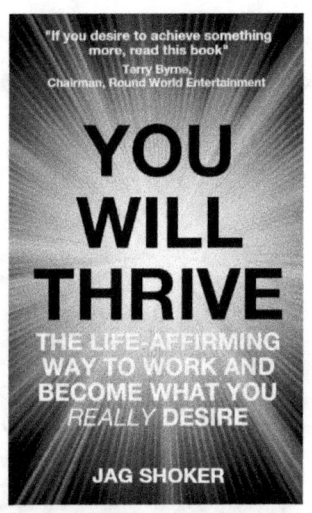

You Will Thrive: The Life-Affirming Way to Work and Become What You Really Desire by Jag Shoker

Have you lost your spark or the passion for what you do? Is your heart no longer in your work or (like so many people) are you simply disillusioned by the frantic race to get ahead in life? Your sense of unease may be getting harder to ignore, and comes from the growing urge to step off the treadmill and pursue a more thrilling *and* meaningful direction in life.

You Will Thrive addresses the subject of modern disillusionment. It is essential reading for people looking to make the most of their talents and be something more in life. Something that matters. Something that makes a difference in the world.

Through six empowering steps, it reveals 'the Way' to boldly follow your heart as it leads you to the perfect opportunities you seek. Through every step, it urges you to put a compelling thought to the test:

You possess the power within you to attract the right people, opportunities, and circumstances that you need to become what you desire.

As you'll discover, if you find the *faith* to act on this power and do the Work required to realise your dream, a testing yet life-affirming path will unfold before you as life *orchestrates* the Way to make it all happen.

The Savvy Traveller Survival Guide by Peter John

Travel is one of our favourite activities. From the hustle of bustle of the mega-cities to sleepy mountain towns to the tranquillity and isolation of tropical islands, we love to get out there and explore the world.

But globe-trotting also comes with its pitfalls. Wherever there are travellers, there are swindlers looking to relieve individuals of their money, possessions and sometimes even more. To avoid such troubles, and to get on with enjoyable and fulfilling trips, people need to get smart. This book shows you how.

The Savvy Traveller Survival Guide offers practical advice on avoiding the scams and hoaxes that can ruin any trip. From no-menu, rigged betting, and scenic taxi tour scams to rental damage, baksheesh, and credit card deceits – this book details scam hotspots, how the scams play out and what you can do to prevent them. The Savvy Traveller Survival Guide will help you develop an awareness and vigilance for high-risk people, activities, and environments.

Forewarned is forearmed!